Disney's

HOW • TO • DRAW

Beauty and the Beast

Illustrated by
David Pacheco
Diana Wakeman

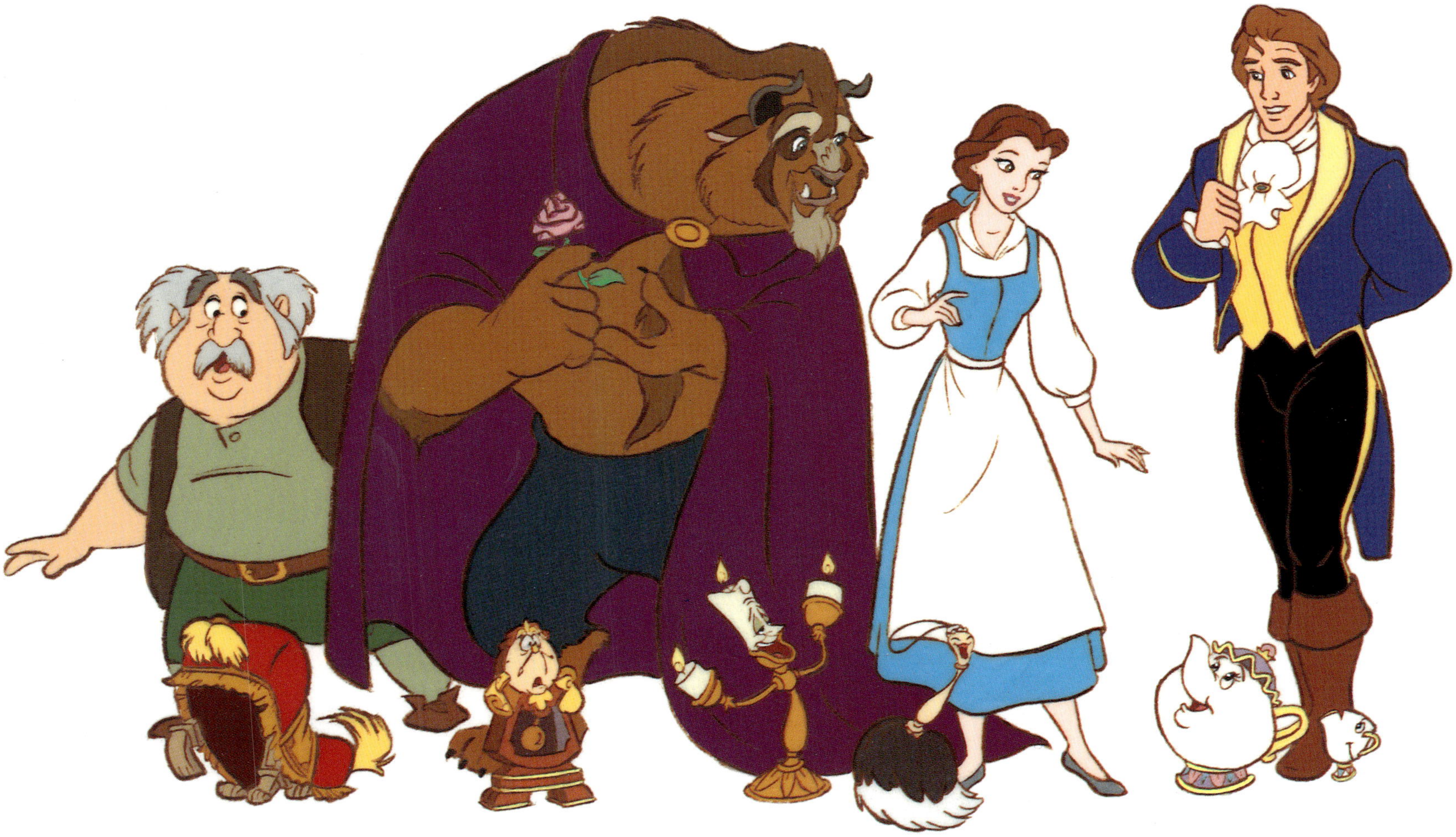

Walter Foster

The Making of *Beauty and the Beast*

The Disney movie *Beauty and the Beast* opened in 1991 to an eager audience. *The Little Mermaid* had remained enormously popular, and *Beauty and the Beast* promised to be even more so. Audiences were not disappointed. The Disney artists' dedication and love for their craft ensured that *Beauty and the Beast* would be animation at its best.

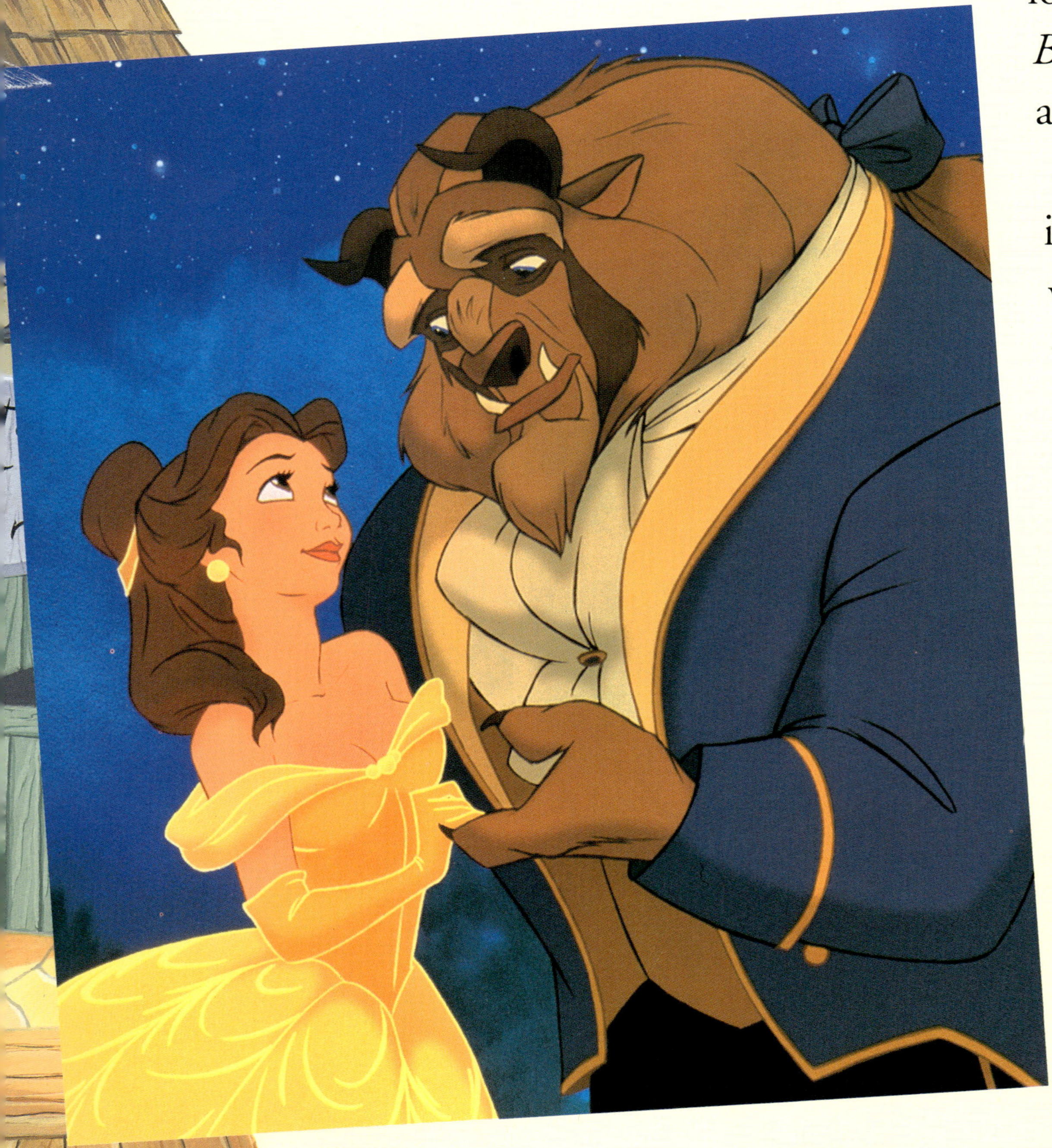

Early during the production, it was acknowledged that music would be the driving force in the re-telling of this classic tale. Musical numbers that would rival Broadway show-stoppers were composed and integrated into the story. After the directors approved the script and songs, it was time for the artists to get to work. Painstaking efforts produced lavish scenes and hours of research resulted in authentic backgrounds and costumes.

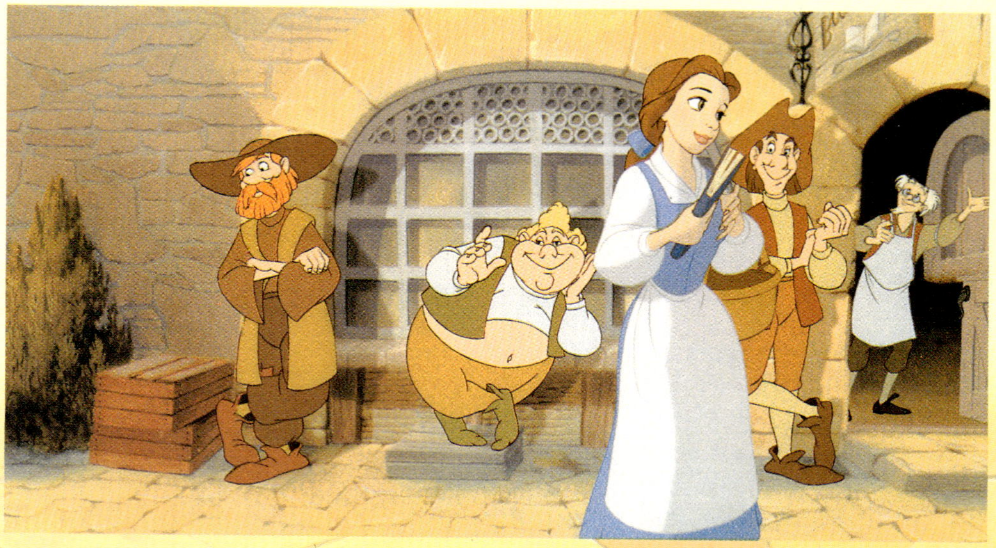

The main characters required the most intensive research. Belle appears twice as often as any other character in the movie, so it was important to get her look right. She is a natural beauty—young, but far from naive. Her healthy coloring comes from an active life, not from cosmetics.

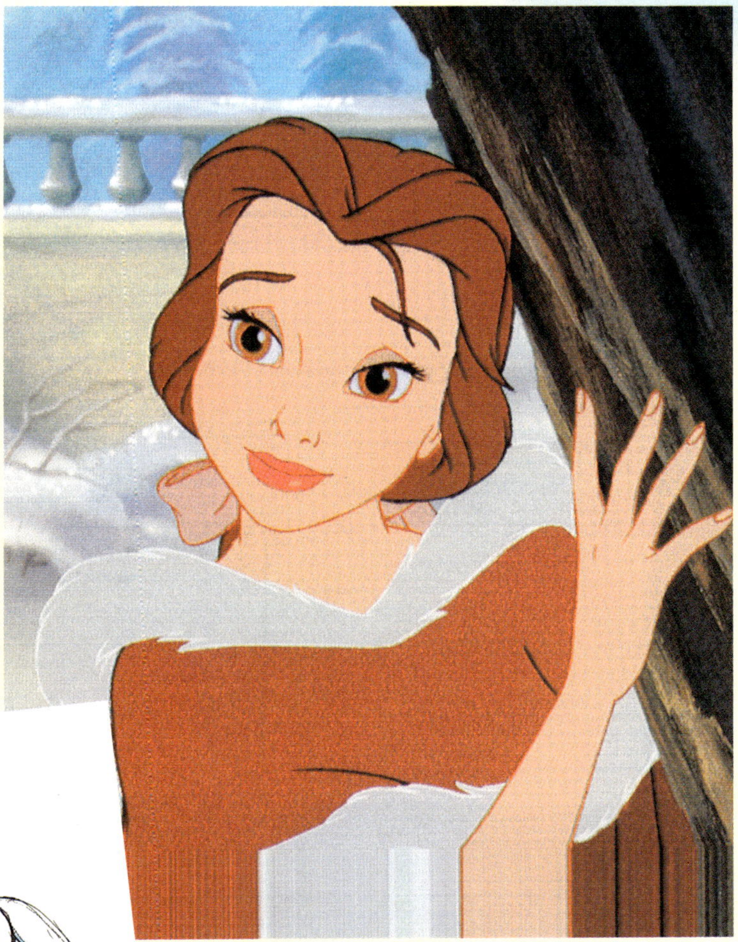

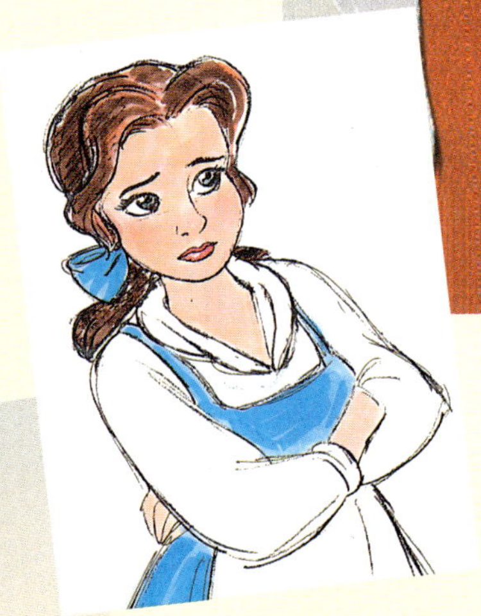

Belle's slightly tilted eyes give her a mature look, especially when compared to such female characters as Wendy from *Peter Pan*, or even Cinderella. And not since *Snow White and the Seven Dwarfs* has Disney featured a dark-haired heroine.

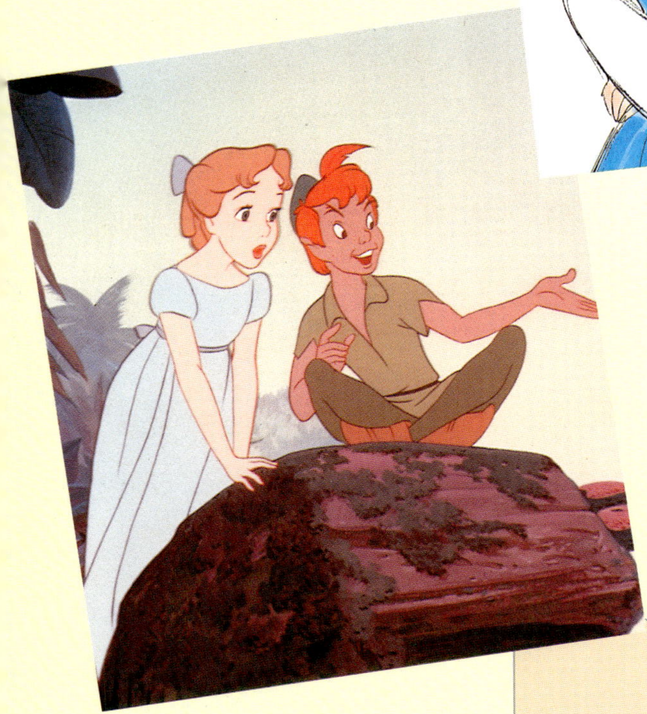

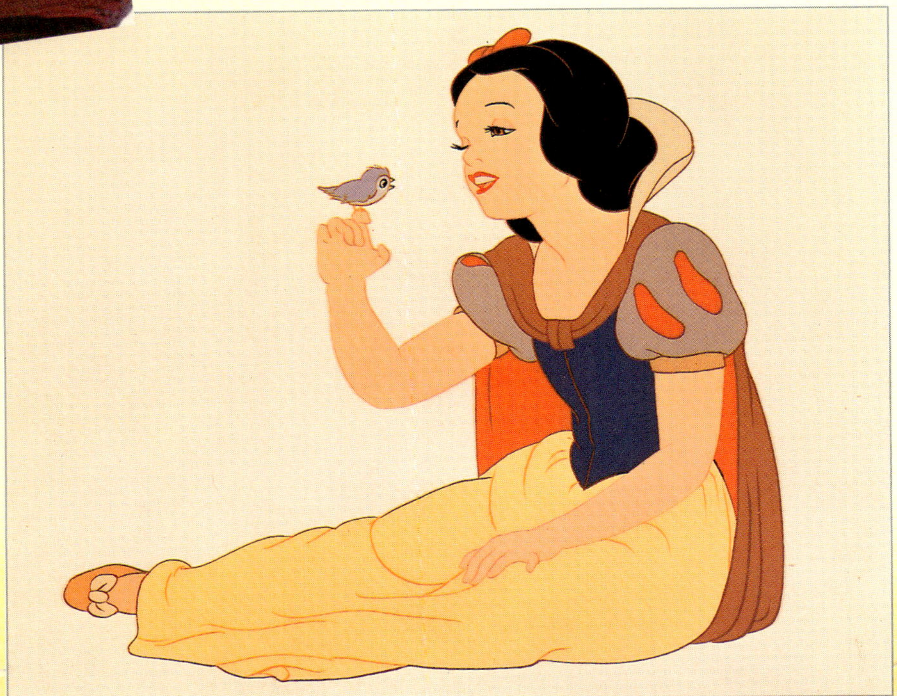

A very different approach was needed in designing the character of the Beast. Animators studied a variety of wild animals to get a sense of what makes them so fearsome. Early sketches of the Beast show him resembling a mandrill, and later, a buffalo. Study the finished Beast and you will see a little of each—with the addition of a boar's tusks, a bear's body and a wolf's tail.

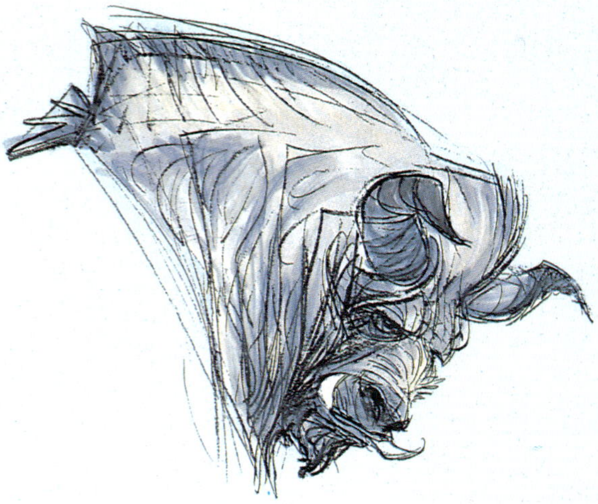

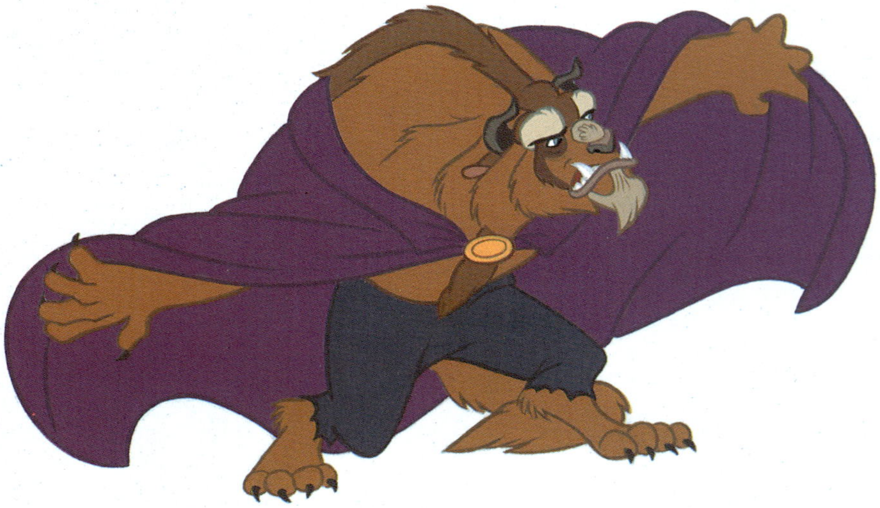

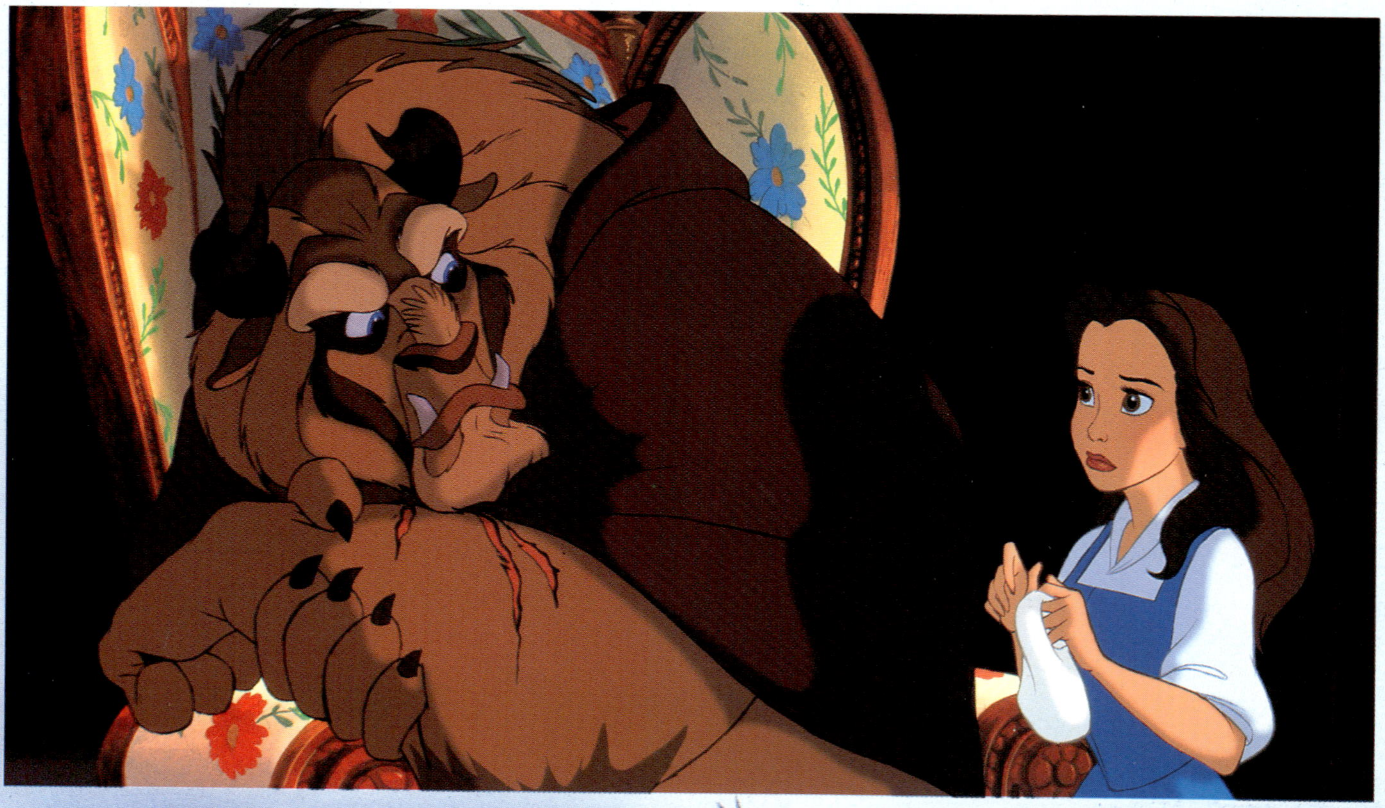

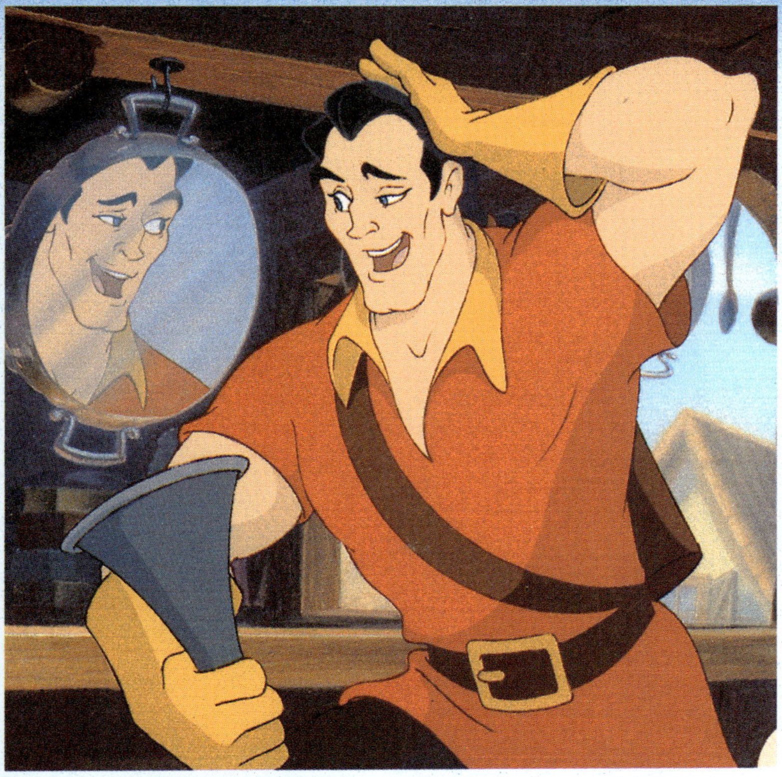

Gaston is easily recognized as an arrogant, conceited male, while his sidekick LeFou (whose name means "the fool" in French) is a hilarious combination of cartoon clowns.

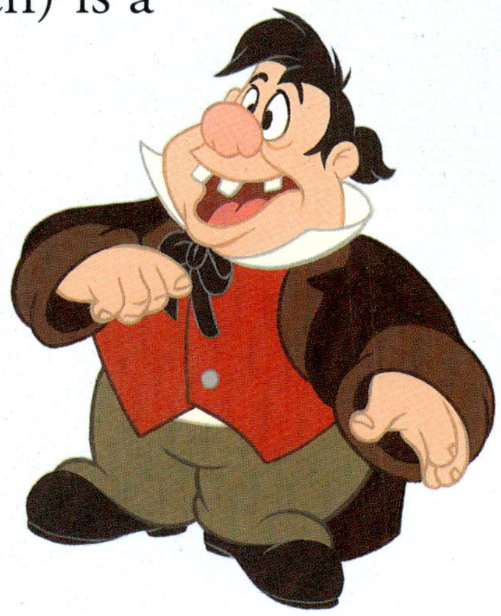

Lumiere, Cogsworth, and Mrs. Potts are more than just household objects. Look carefully at their faces—they are far more human than anything else.

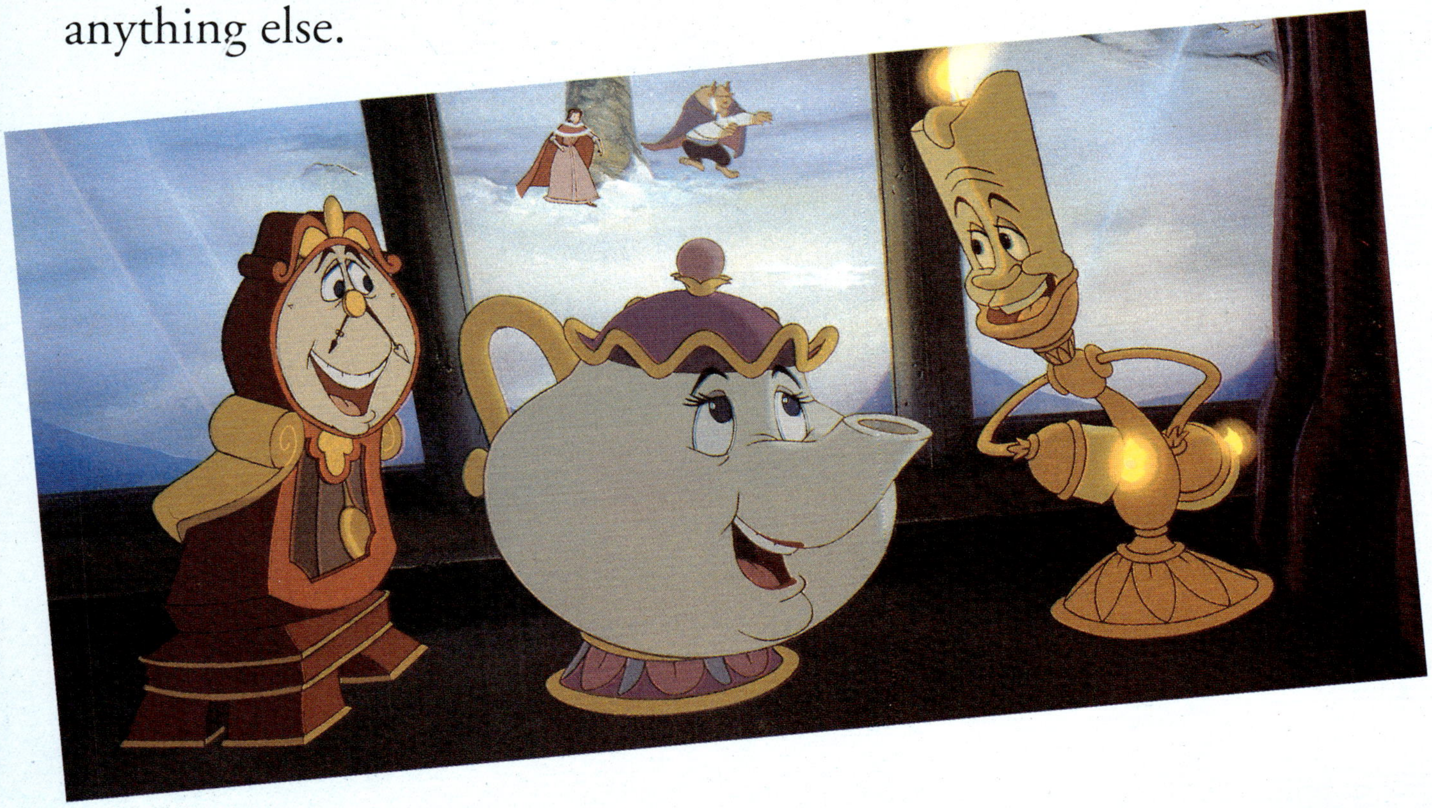

As time goes on, the Disney studios will undoubtedly produce other animated masterpieces. But *Beauty and the Beast*, the "tale as old as time," can never be surpassed in the hearts of the artists who created it.

Drawing Techniques

Drawing Belle and her friends can be fun and rewarding. With a little patience and practice, you will soon be producing successful drawings of your own.

Most characters are based on simple round and oval shapes. Using a light, continuous motion, sketch around and around until you've made a circle or oval that is the correct shape. Also practice drawing curves with smooth strokes. You may then erase any stray lines for a clean look. Try sketching a variety of sizes, or join shapes together to create new shapes.

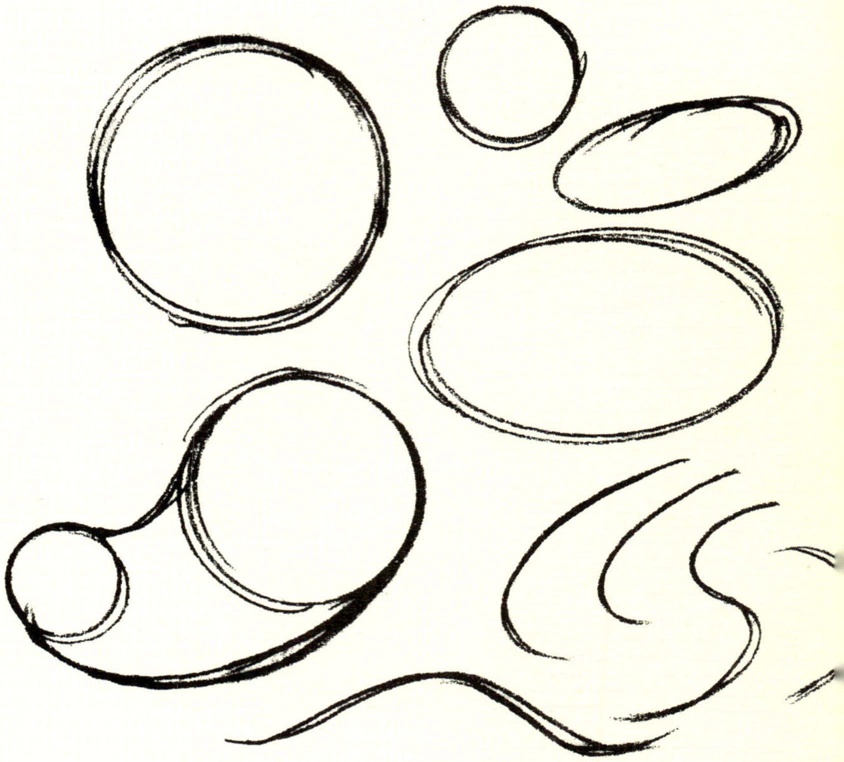

One of the most important things to remember is to begin with a line of action. Draw a ball for the head and a curving line to represent the body. This is what gives your character movement and life. The line of action should flow naturally and smoothly.

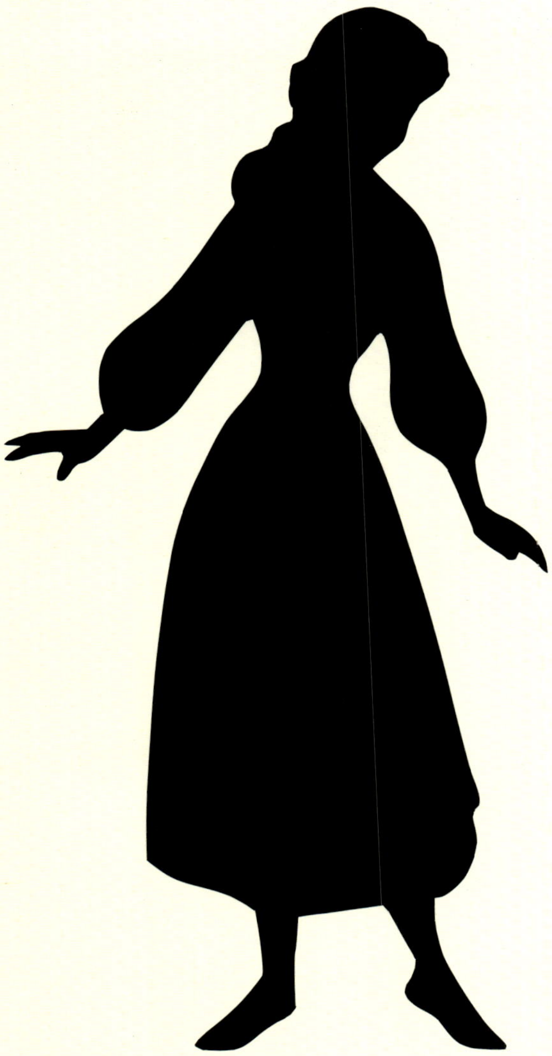

It's useful to transfer the outline of your drawing onto tracing paper. This gives you a silhouette that reflects the character's proportions and shows if you have created a clear, strong pose. A good silhouette helps toward a good finished drawing.

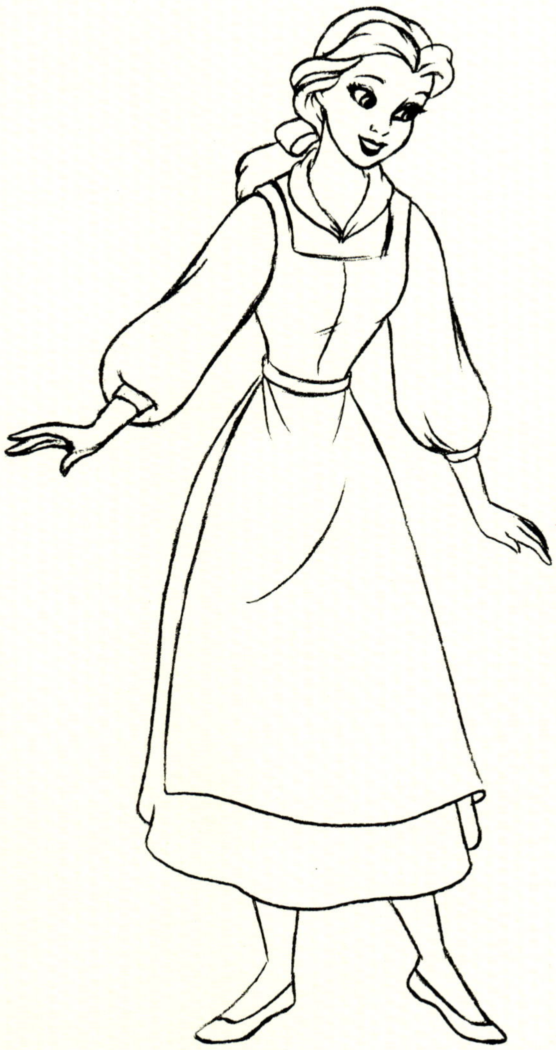

Once you've drawn your character, carefully erase the line of action and other construction lines to clean up your drawing. Now you're ready to color Belle.

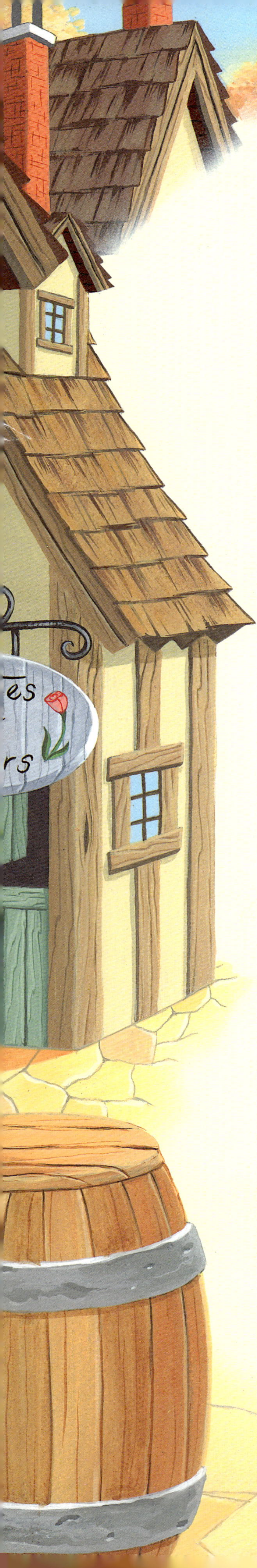

Belle's Head

In this front view of Belle's head, notice how soft curves create her simple beauty.

1

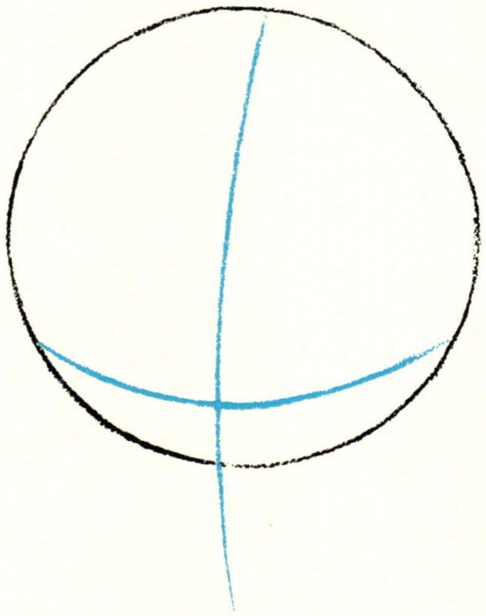

2

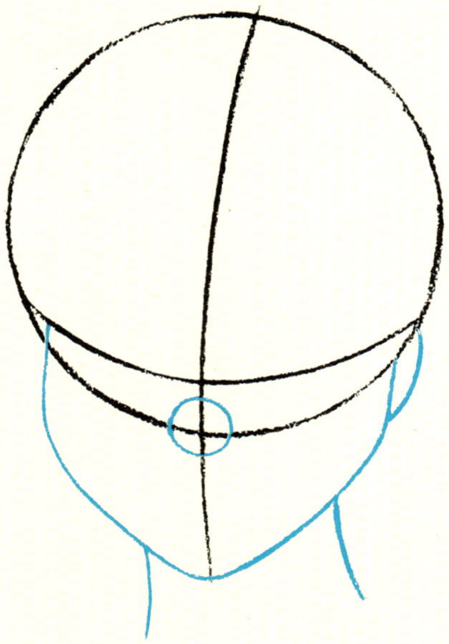

Belle's eyes are set wide apart and tilt slightly up.

3

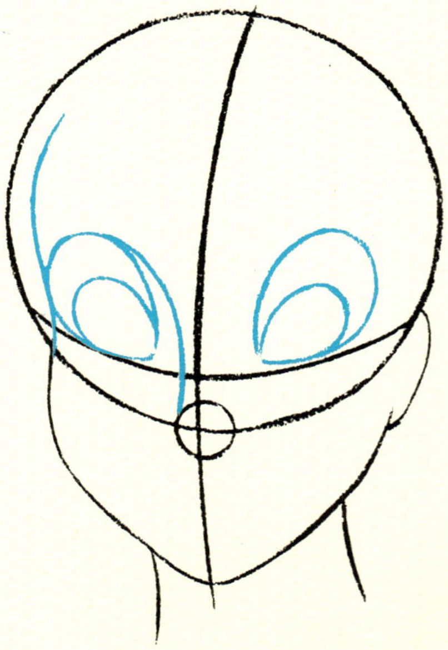

6

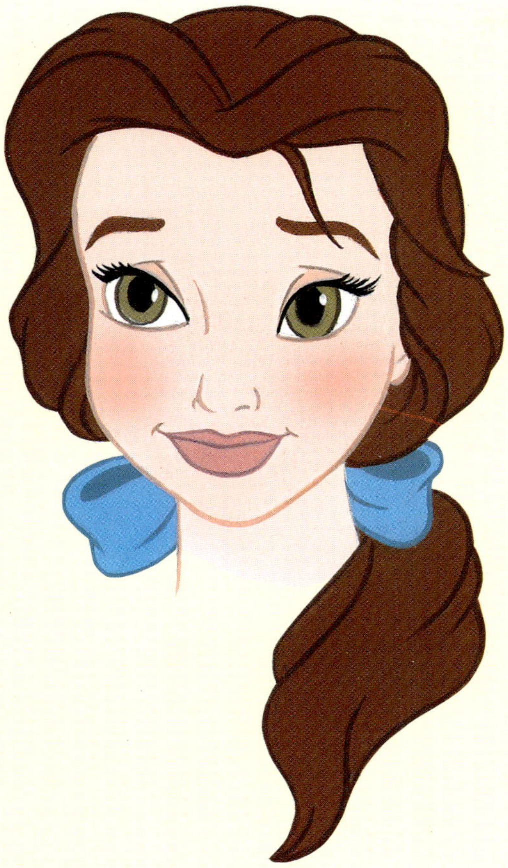

5

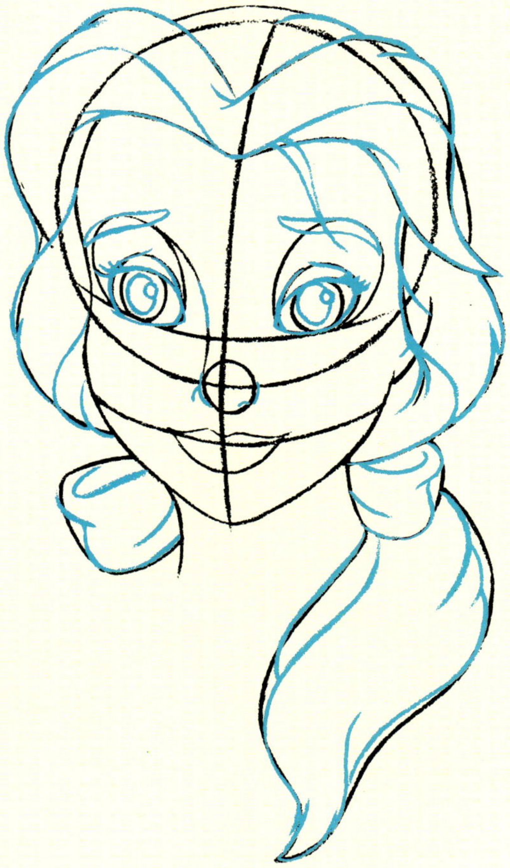

4

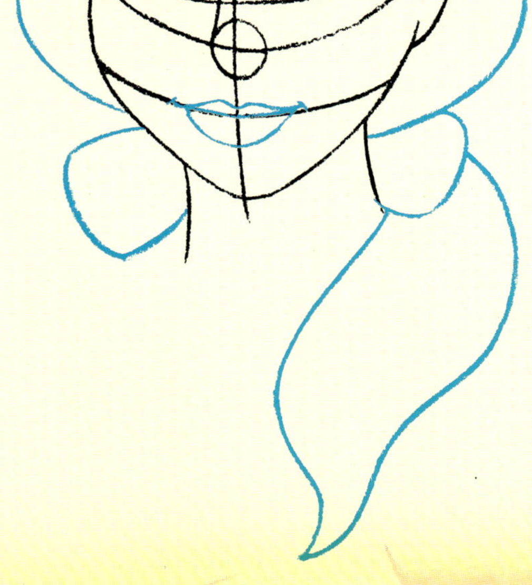

Belle, Expressions

Belle's love of books makes her yearn for faraway places and adventures. Knowing her traits will help you draw Belle in a variety of moods and expressions.

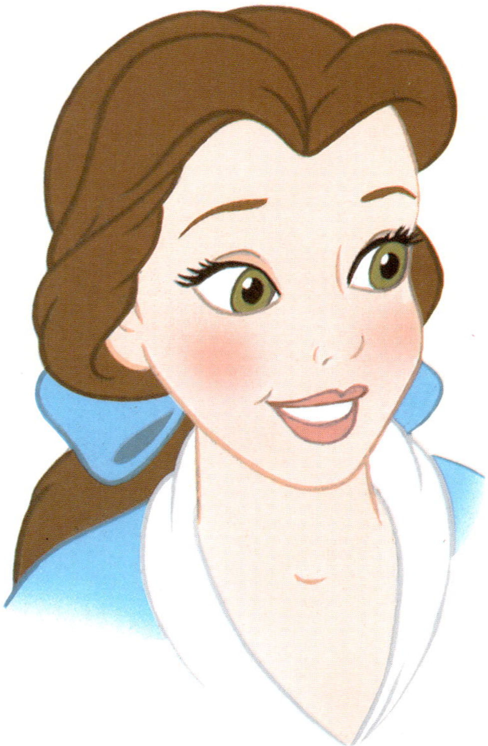

amused

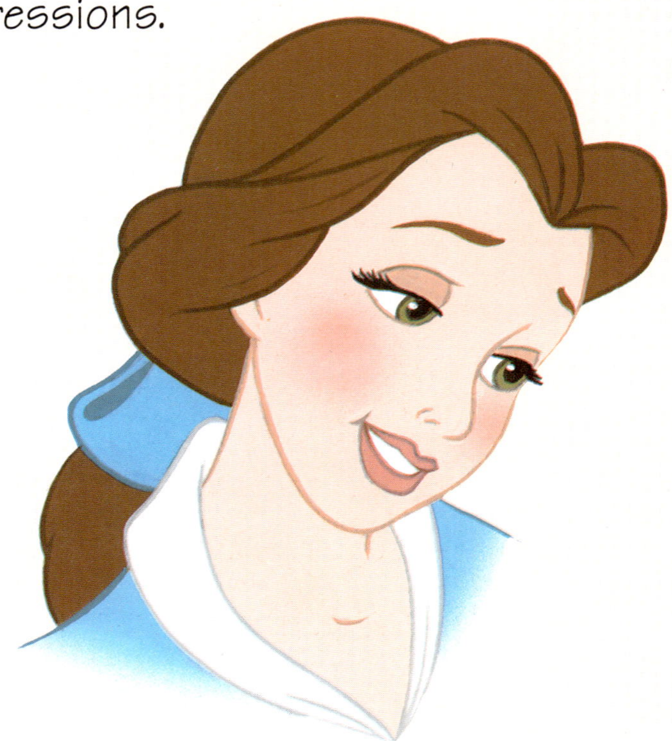

caring

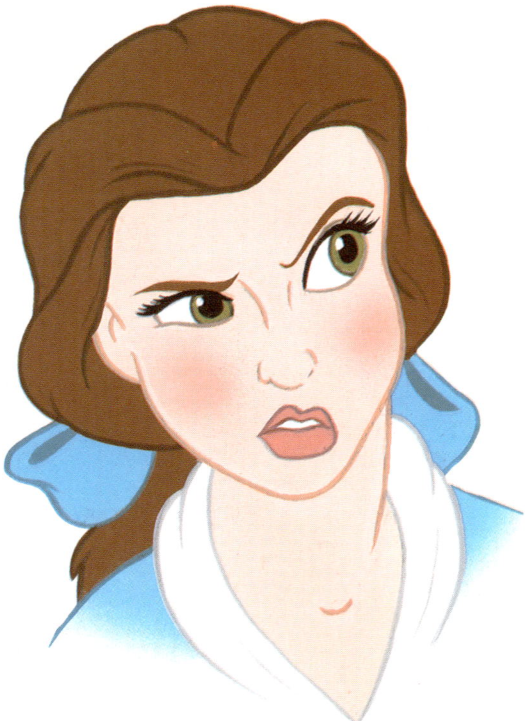

skeptical

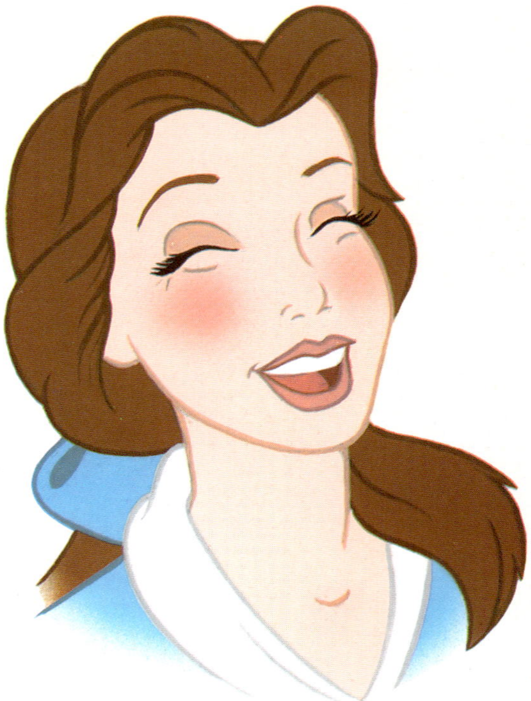

happy

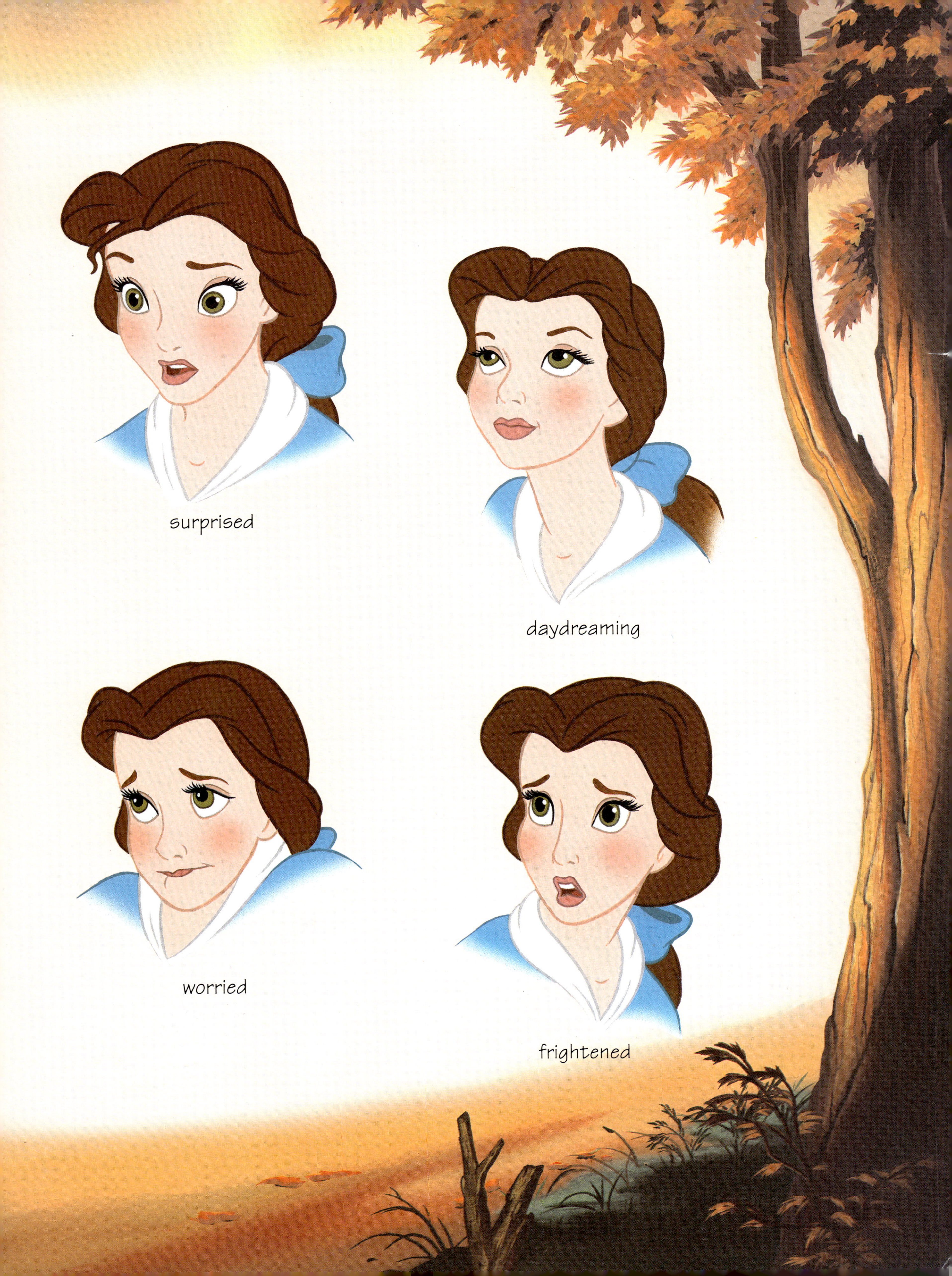
surprised
daydreaming
worried
frightened

Belle, Full Body

Belle is a simple country girl, with a natural beauty that is as much inner goodness as it is looks. Try to think of her as a dancer. Here's how to draw her complete figure.

1

2

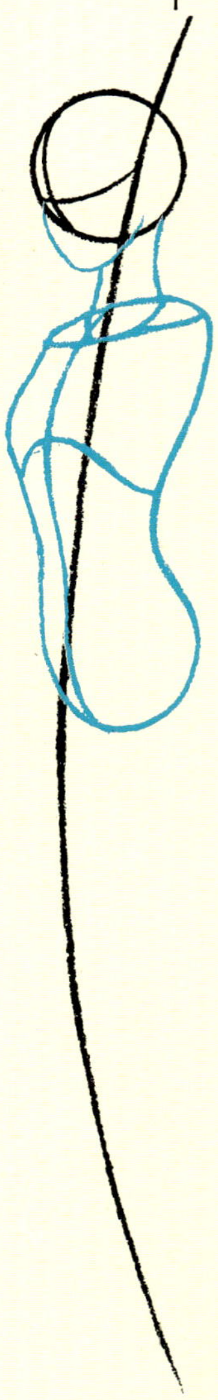

3

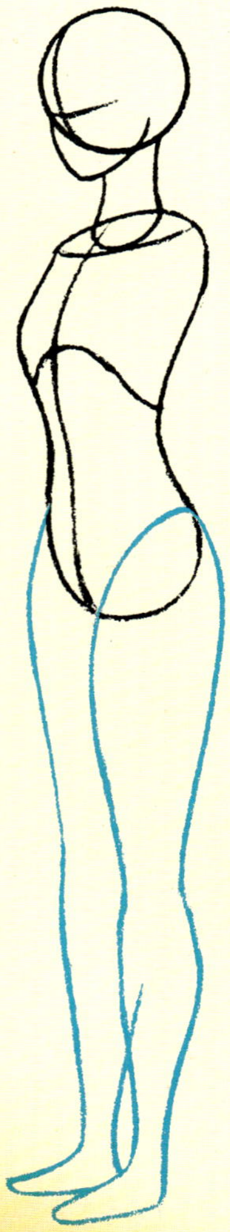

4

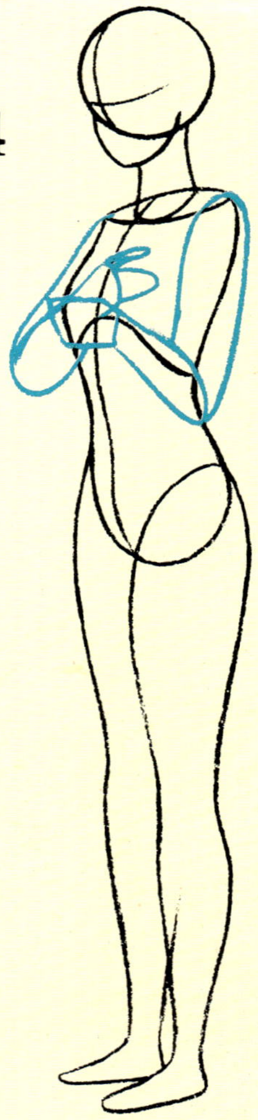

Keep Belle very graceful and tall, with a tapered waist and long, slender legs.

5

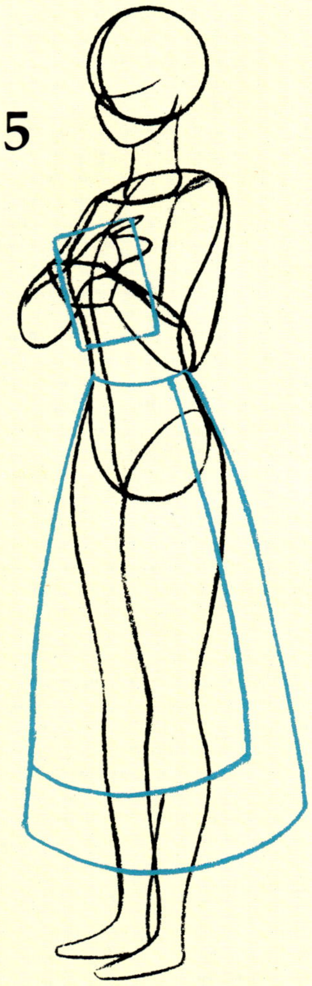

6

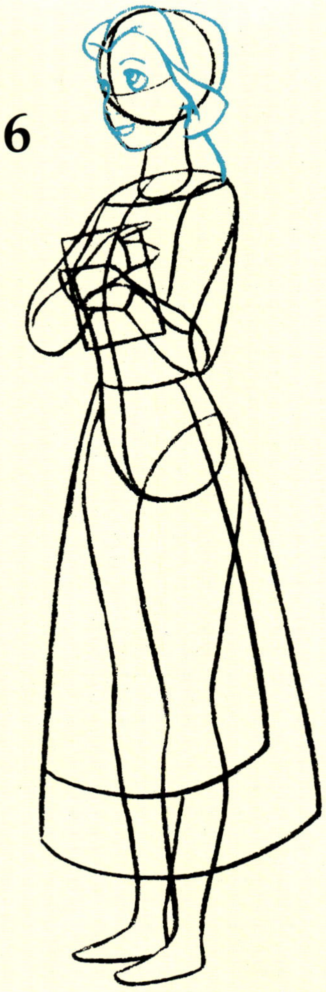

7

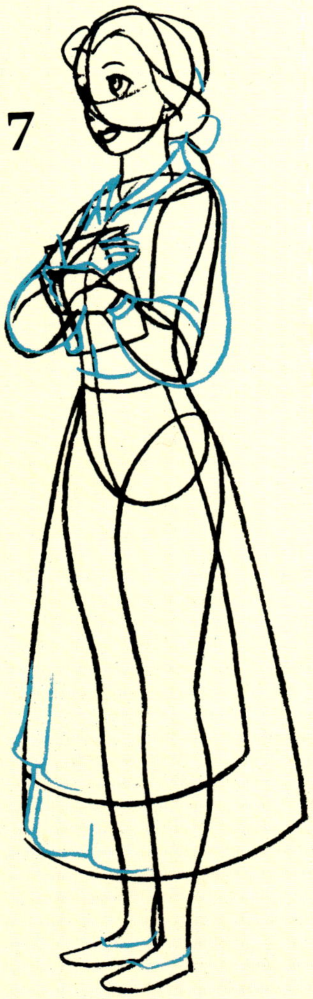

8

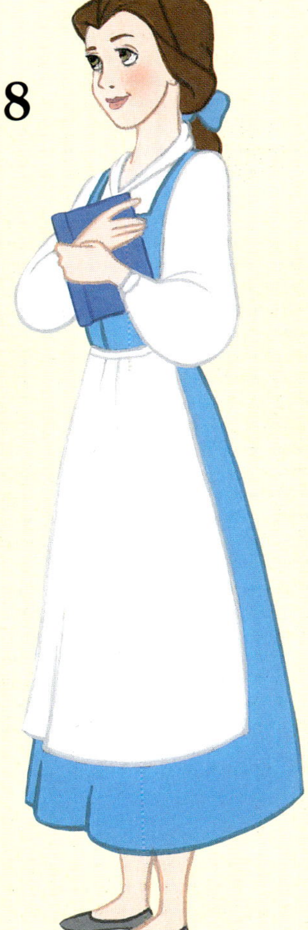

Belle, Action Poses

Now that you've learned to draw Belle's face and body, you can really bring her to life in these action poses.

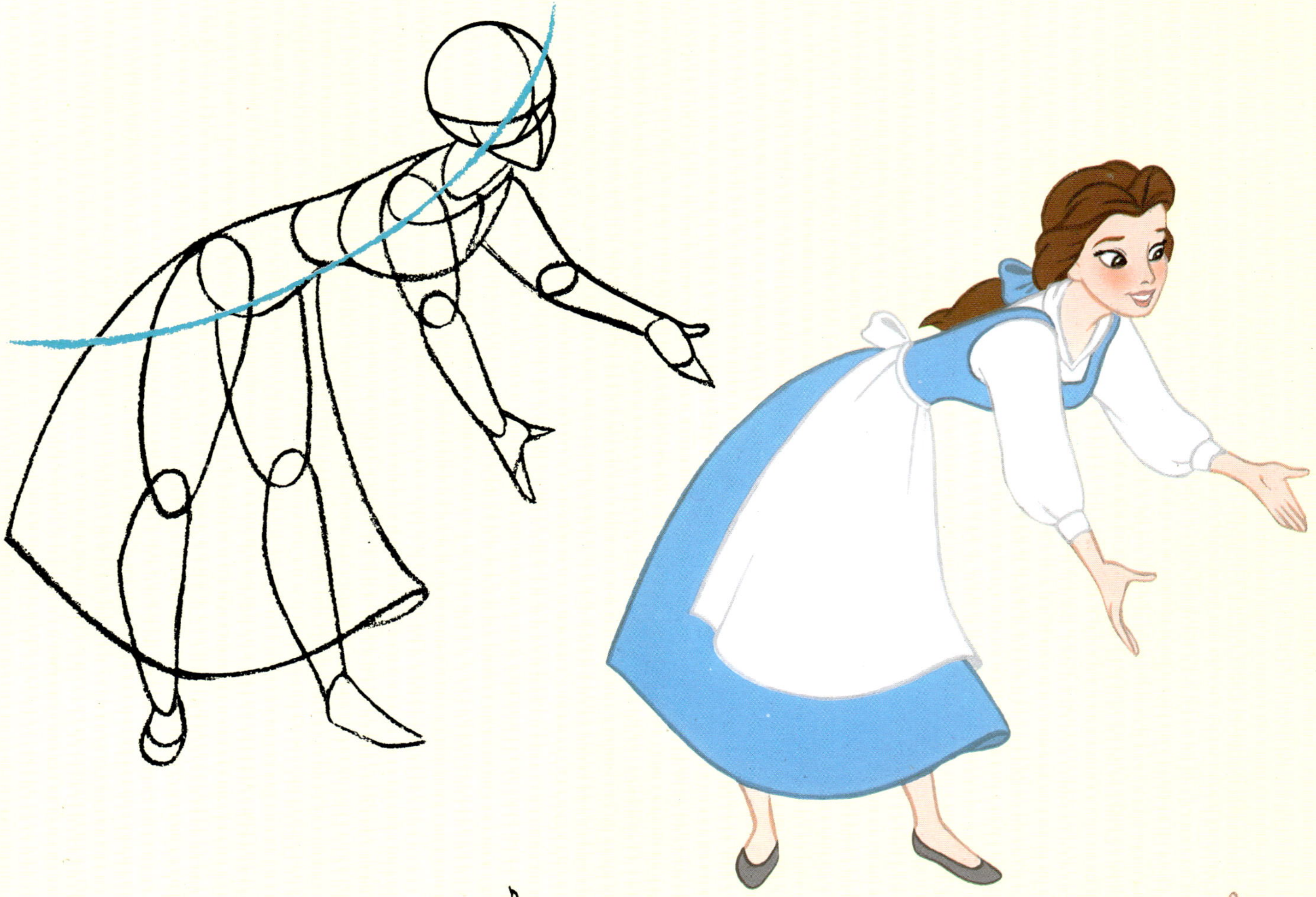

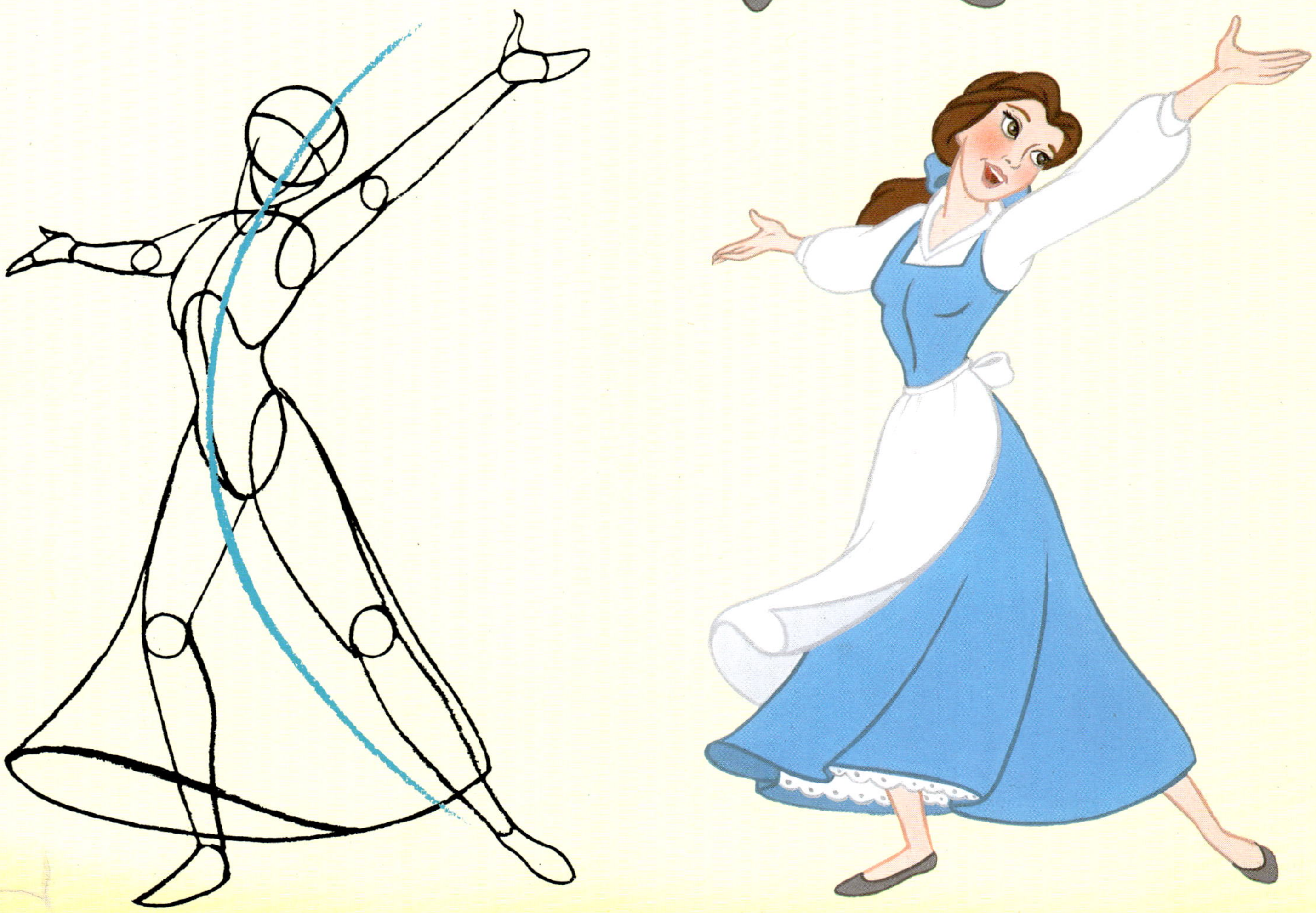

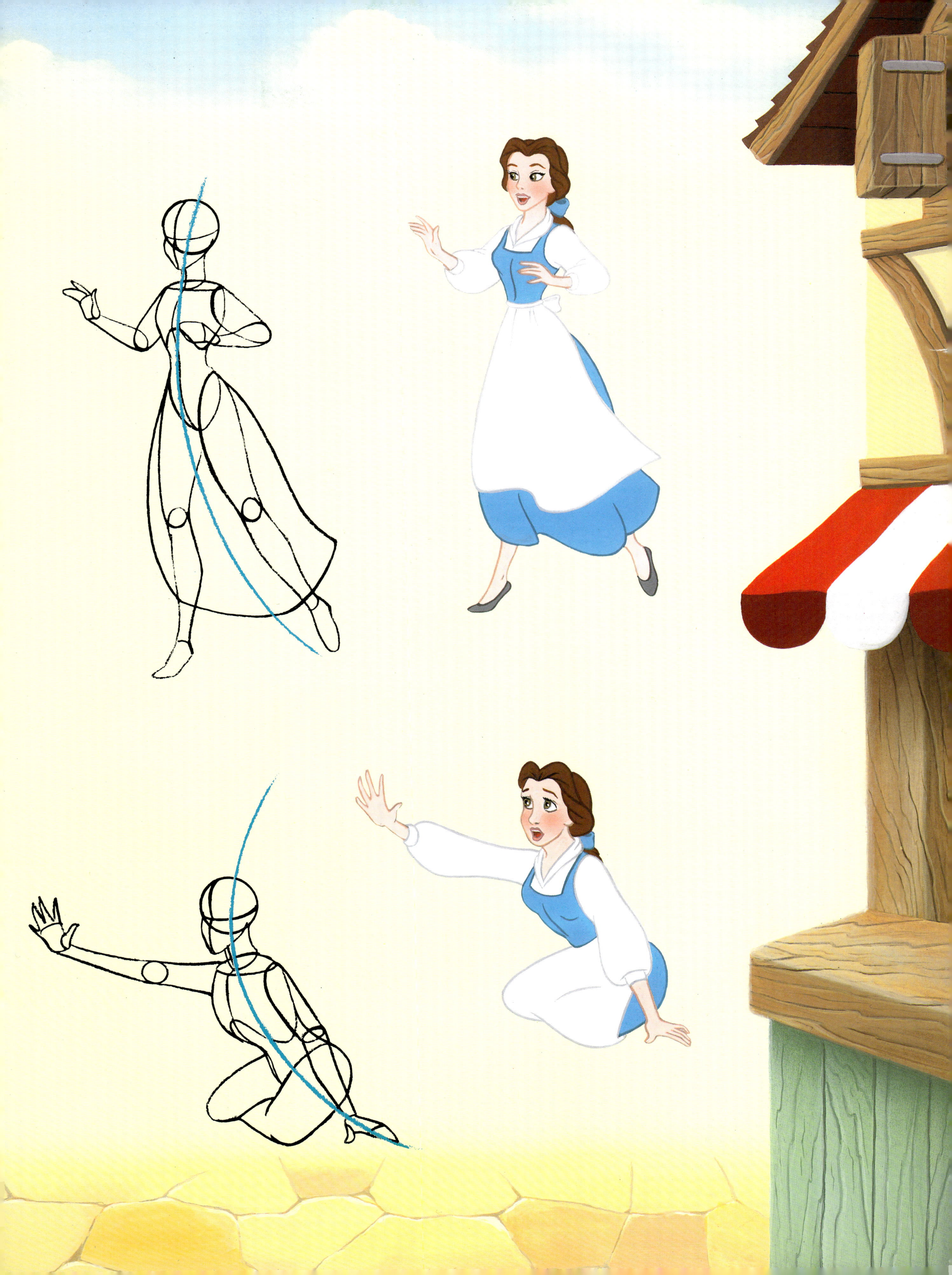

The Beast's Head

The Beast is a combination of many wild animals. But underneath that savage exterior is a frightened young man. Follow the steps and see the depth, form, and structure as you draw the Beast's head.

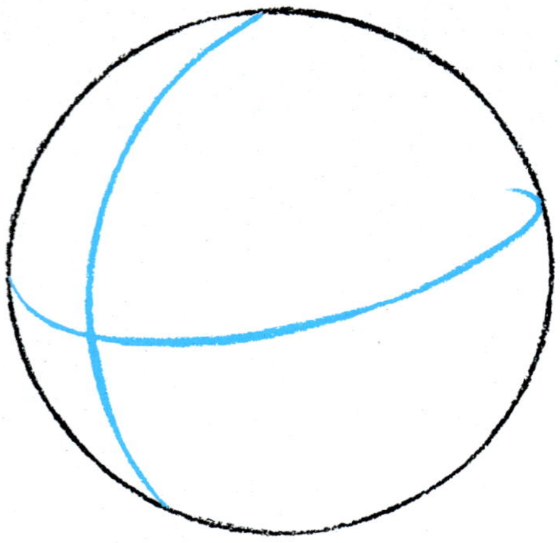

1

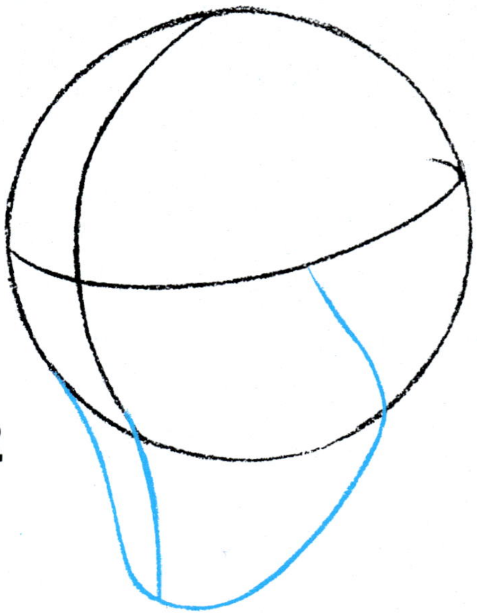

2

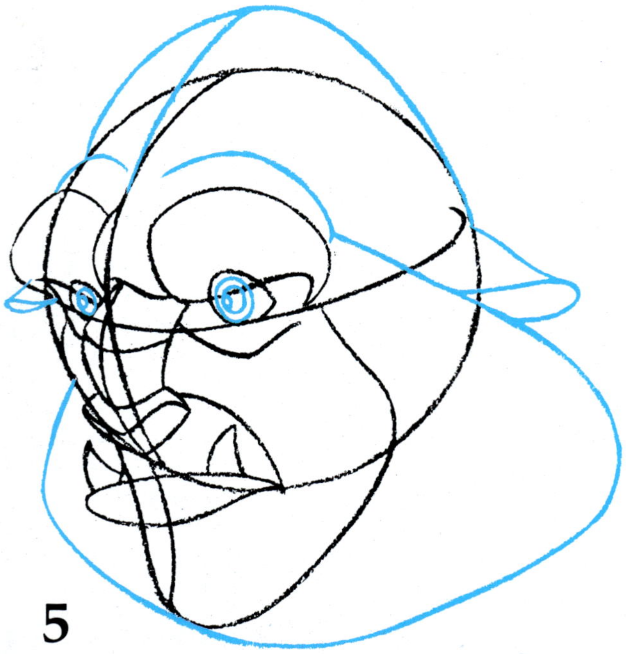

5

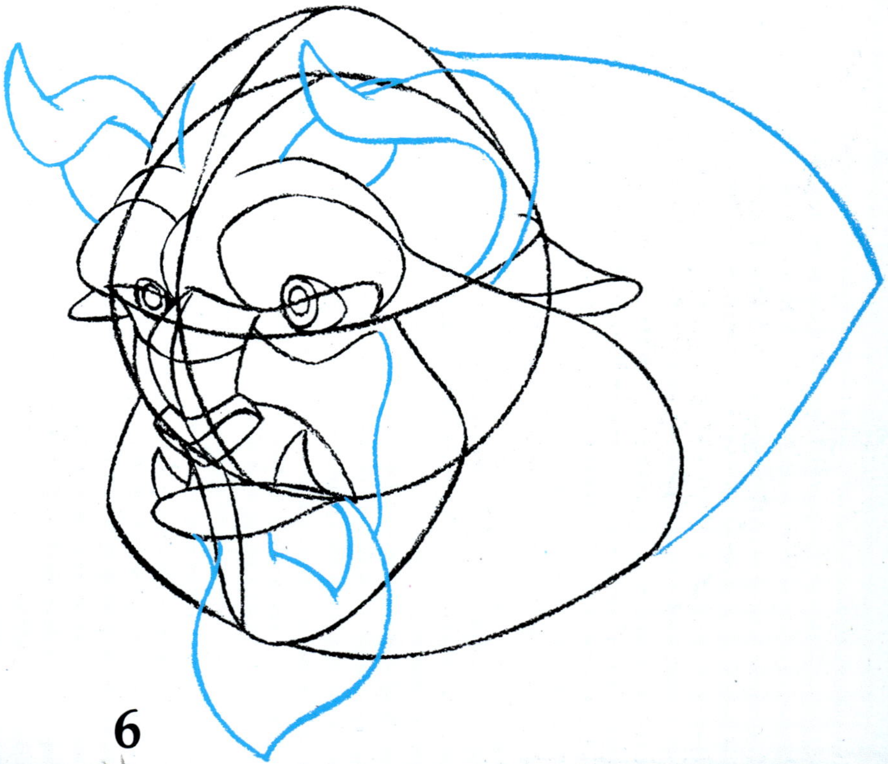

6

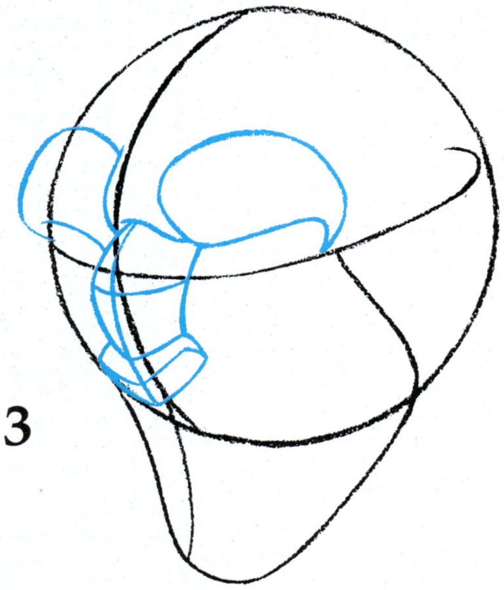

3

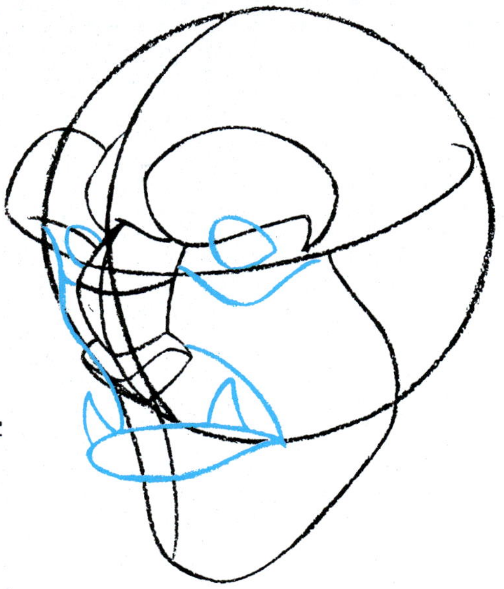

4

Use short, rough strokes for Beast's fur, and careful, detailed lines for his face.

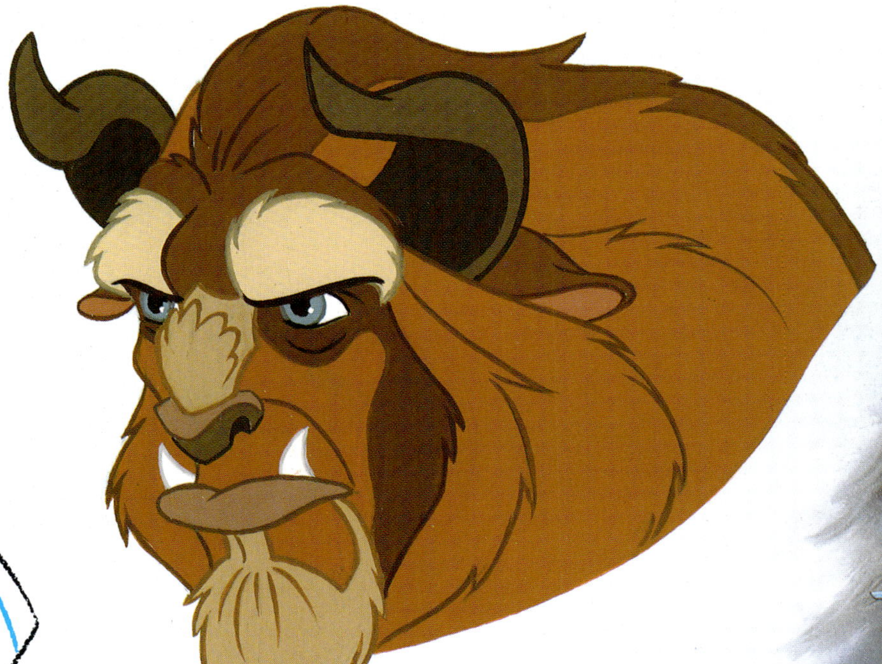

8

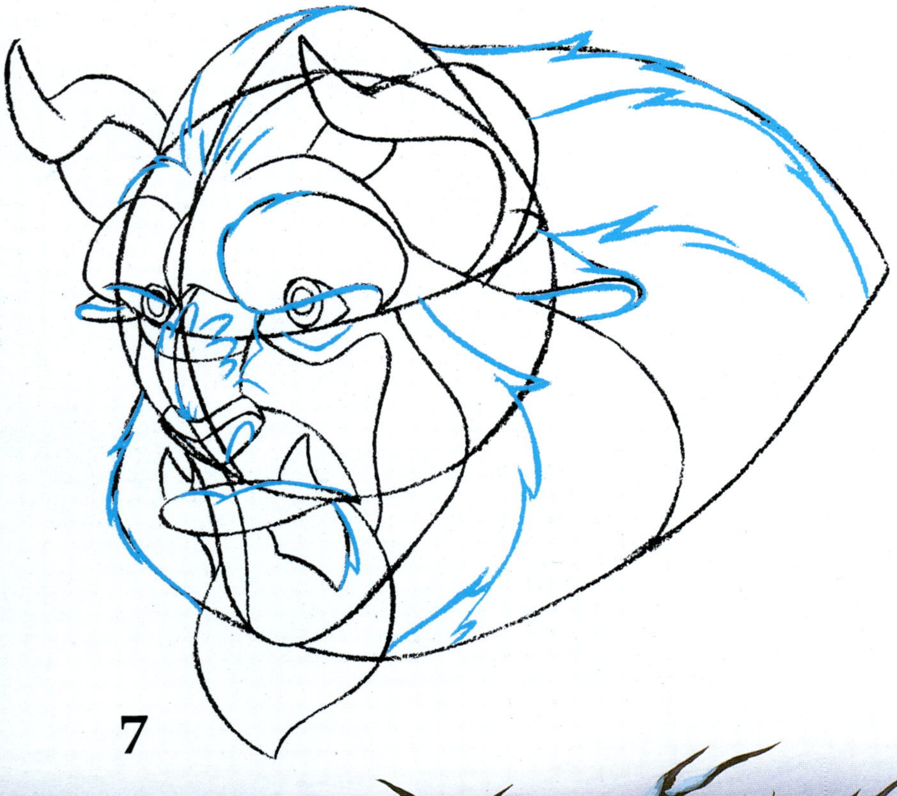

7

The Beast, Expressions

Even a Beast has feelings! Knowing his personality will help you make him more believable.

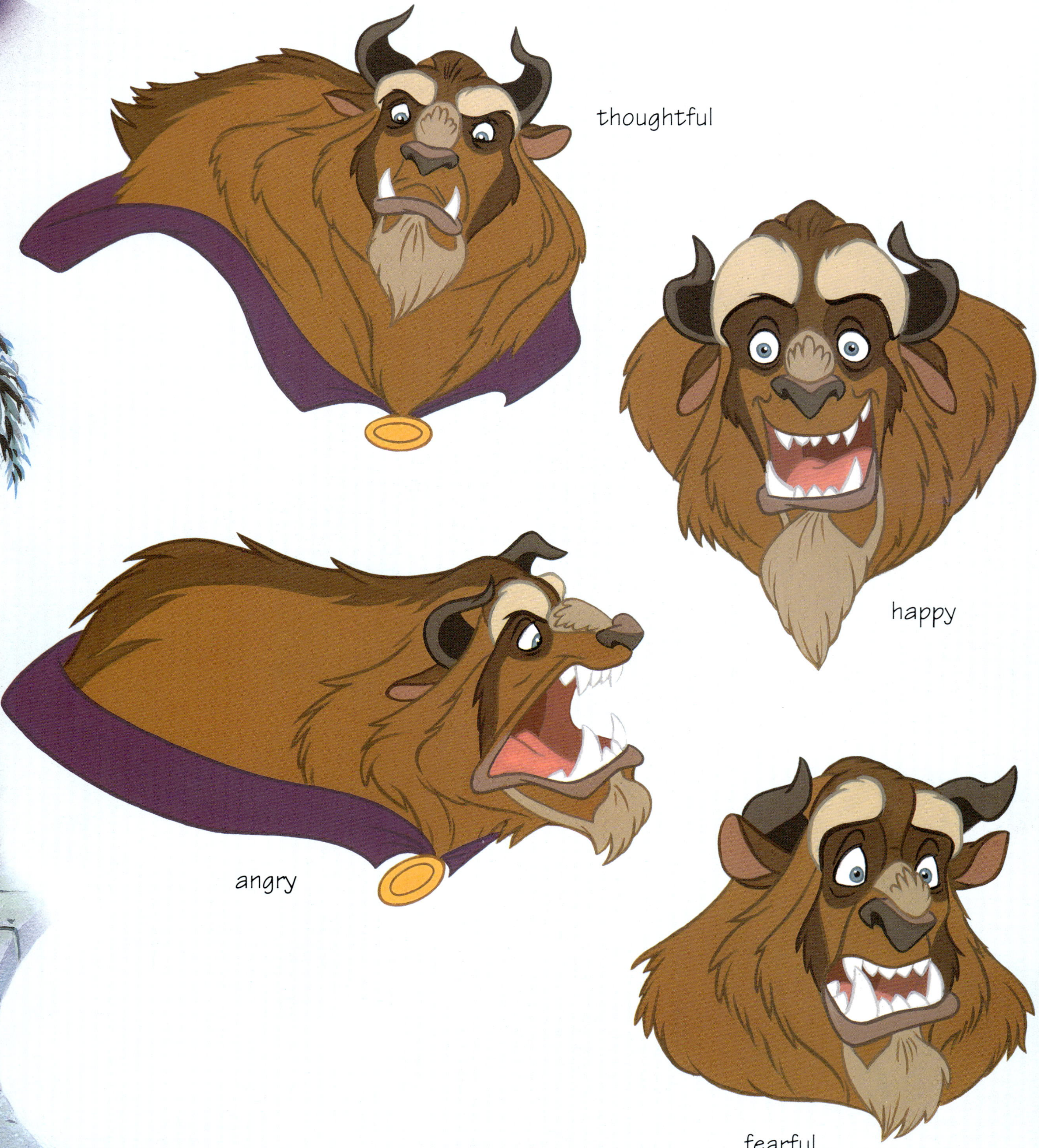

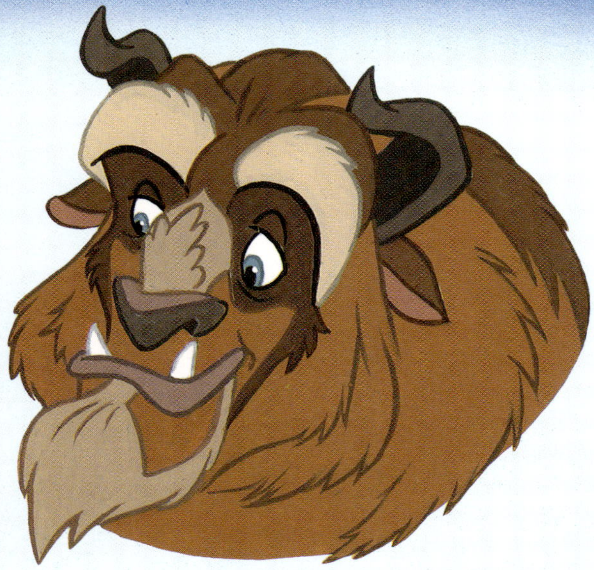

loving

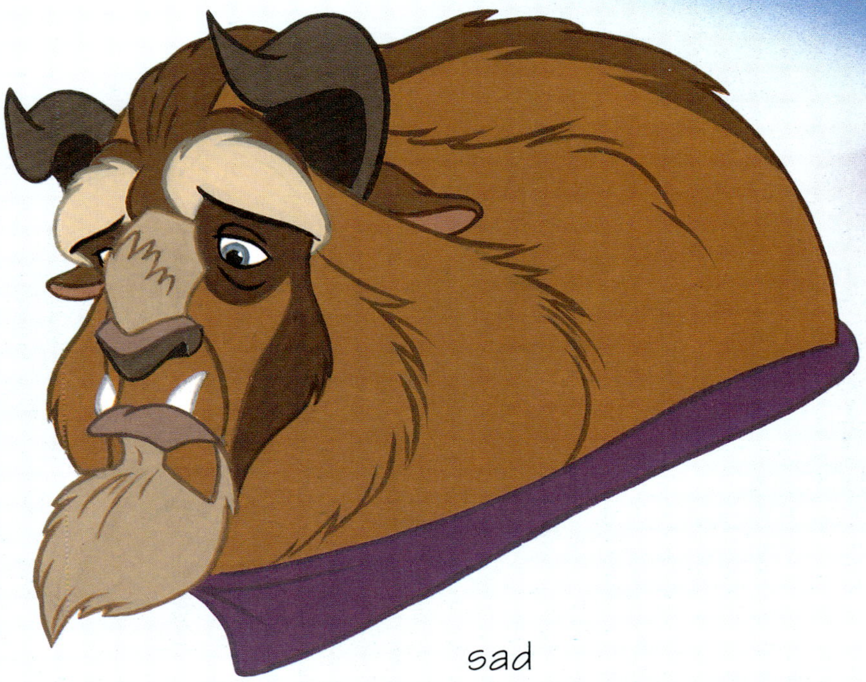

sad

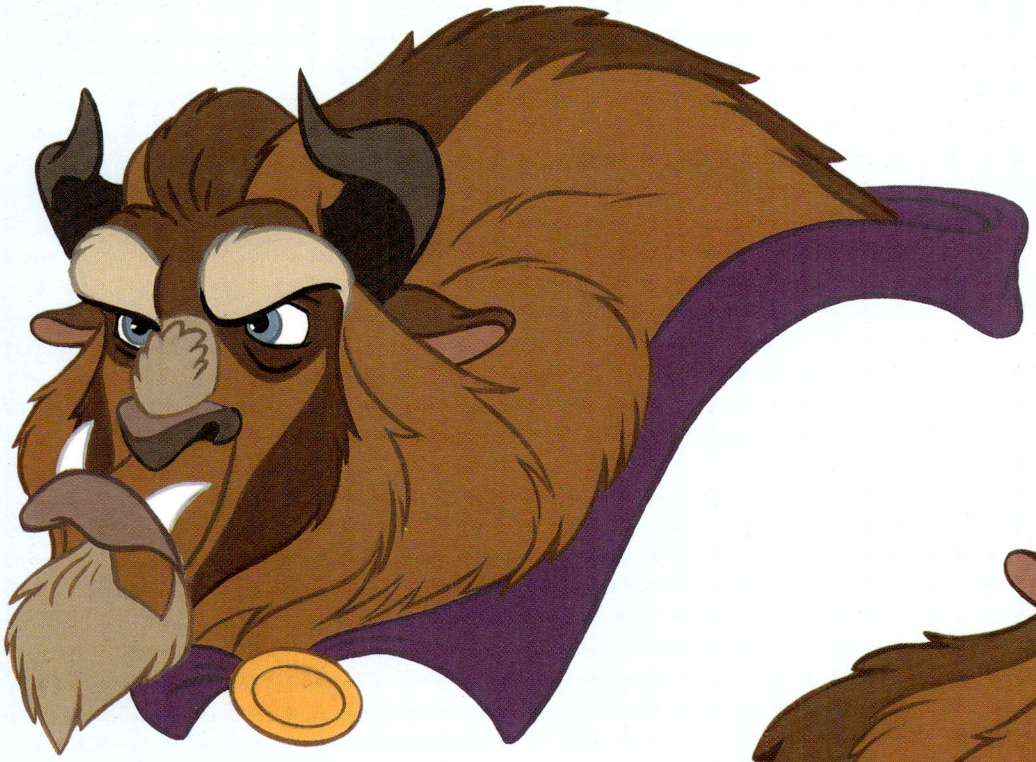

wounded

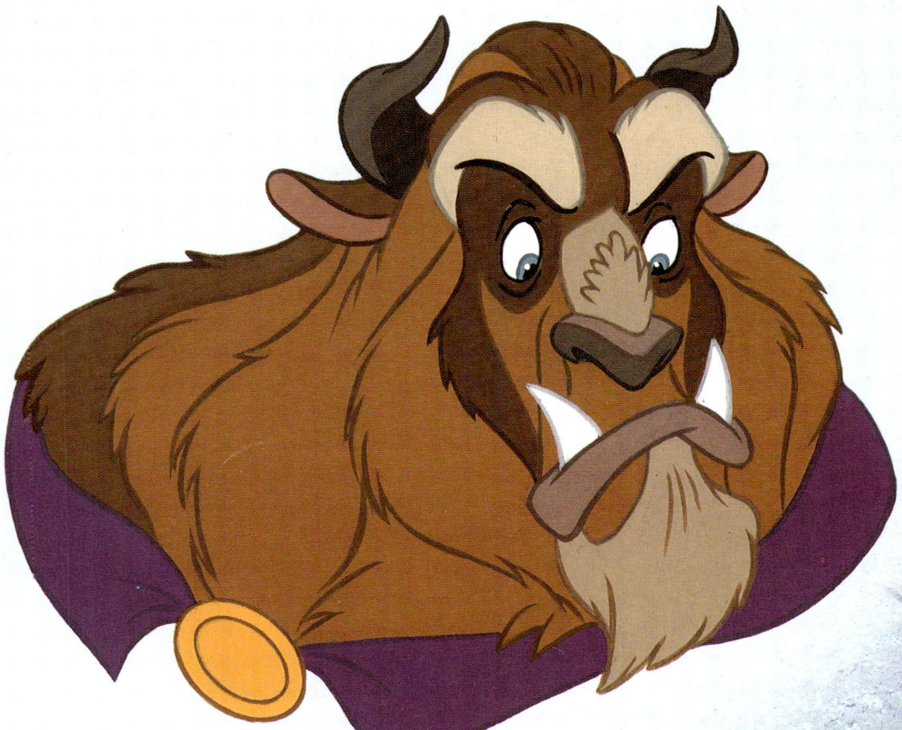

sulking

The Beast, Full Body

At first glance, the Beast may look like a difficult character to draw. Study his proportions and note the various components that make up his frame.

1

2

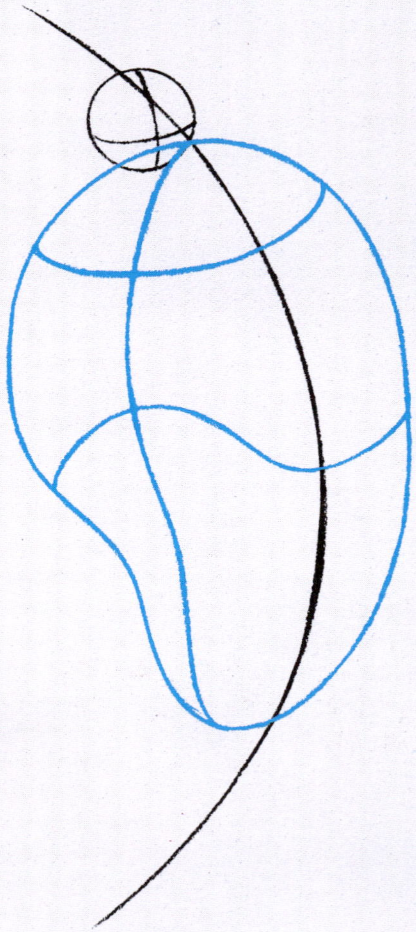

The ball of the Beast's head is small in relation to the mass of his body.

5

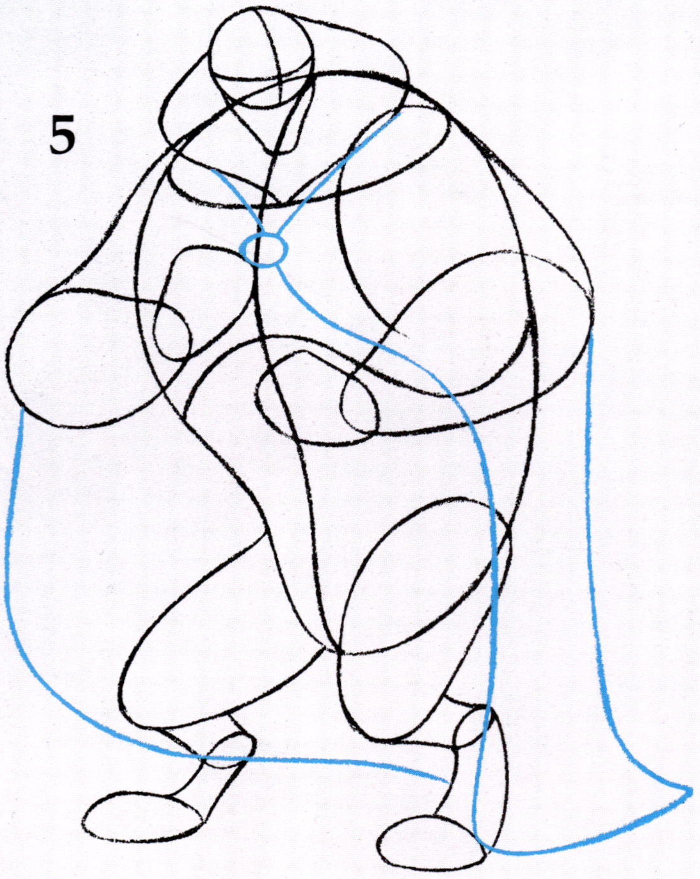

6

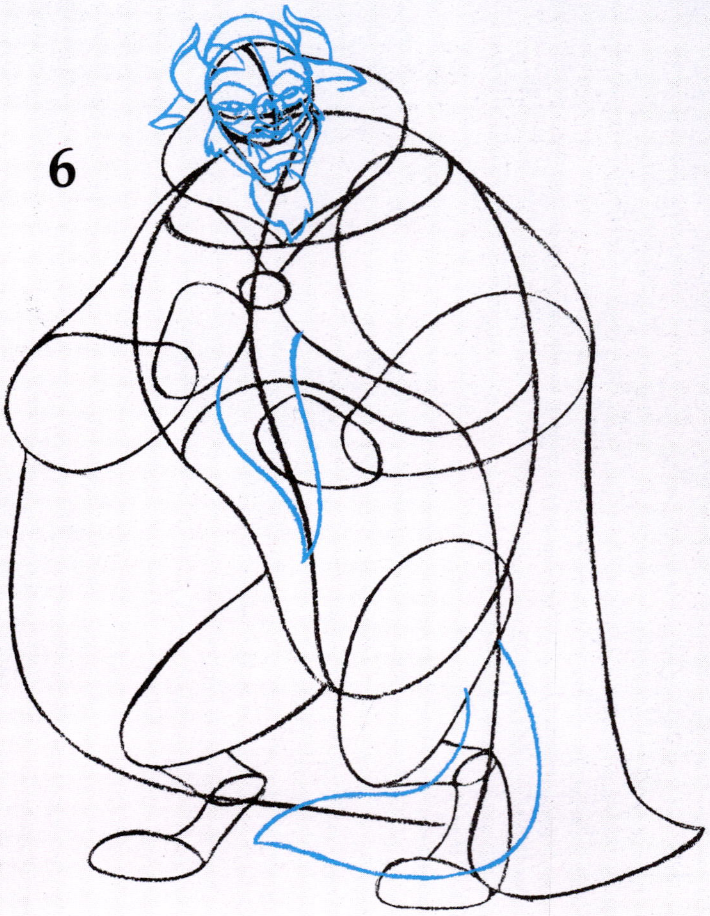

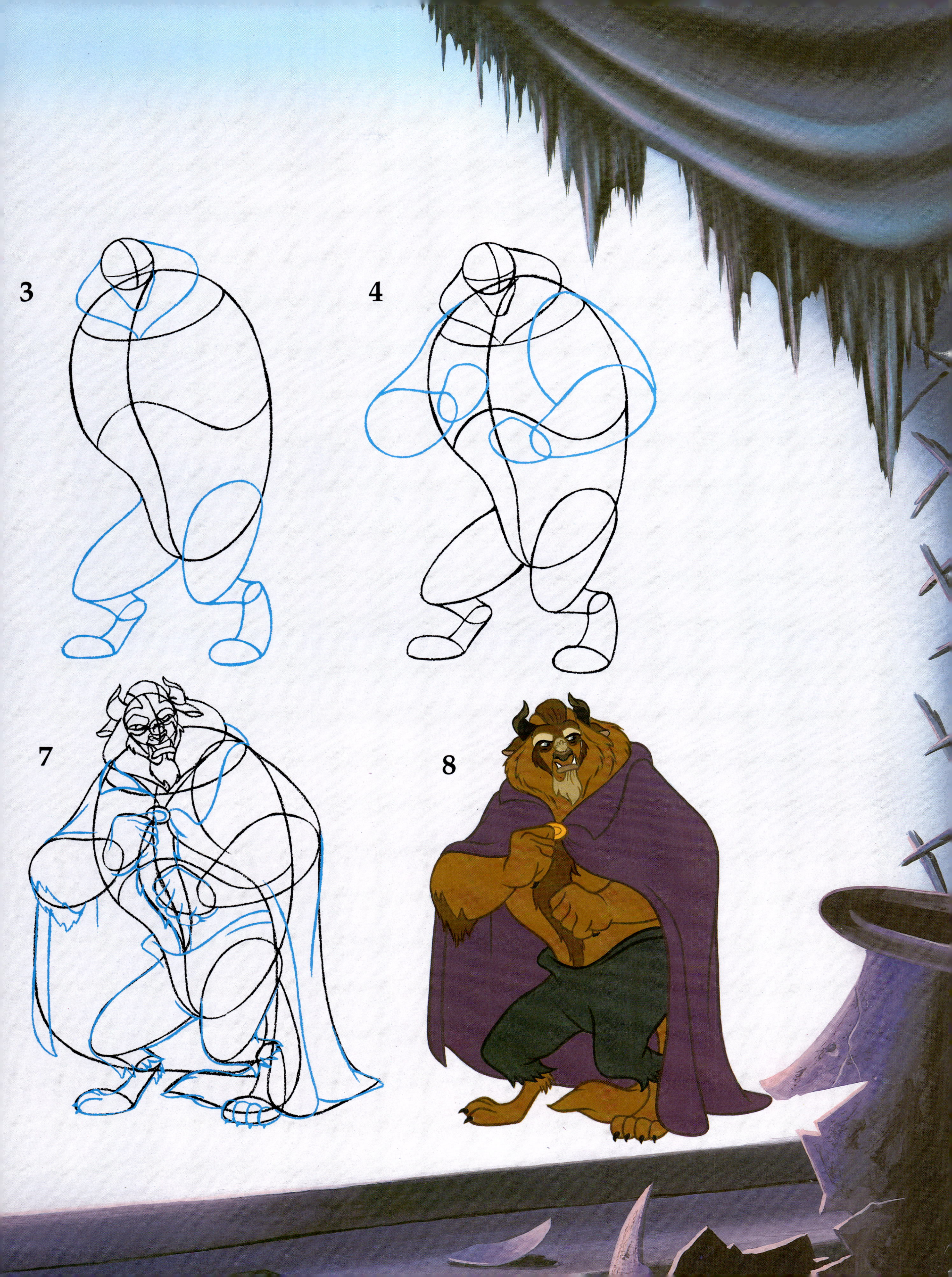
3
4
7
8

The Beast, Action Poses

The Beast has a keen intelligence and a powerful body.
Show this combination when drawing him in these action poses.

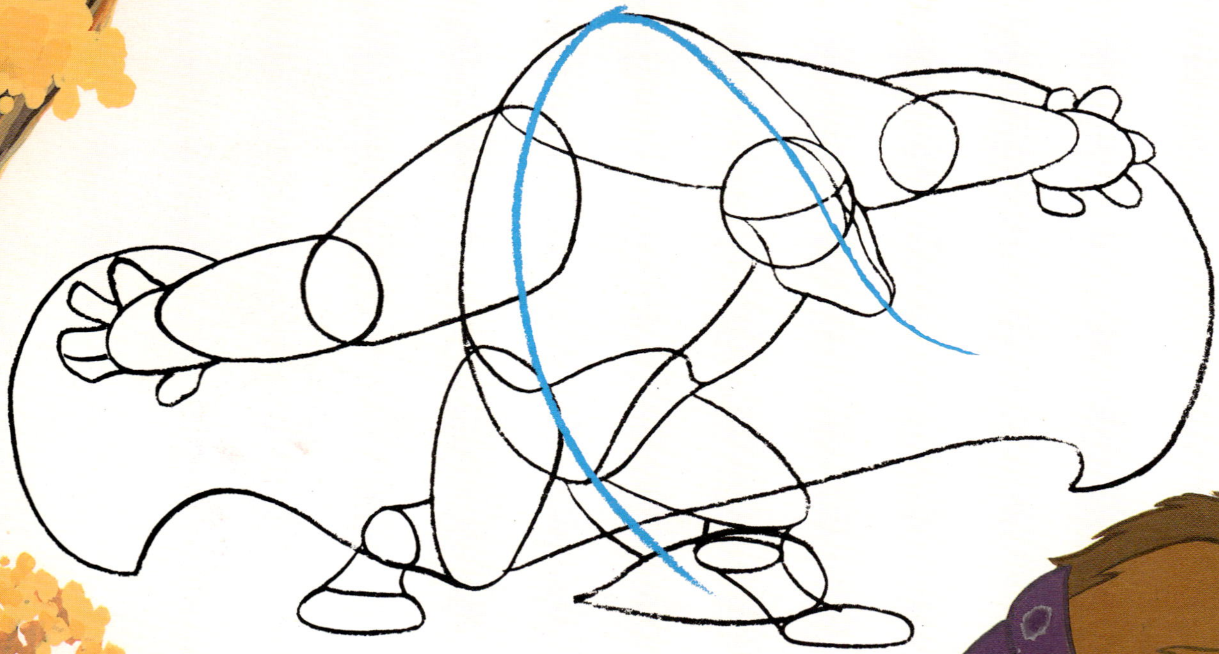

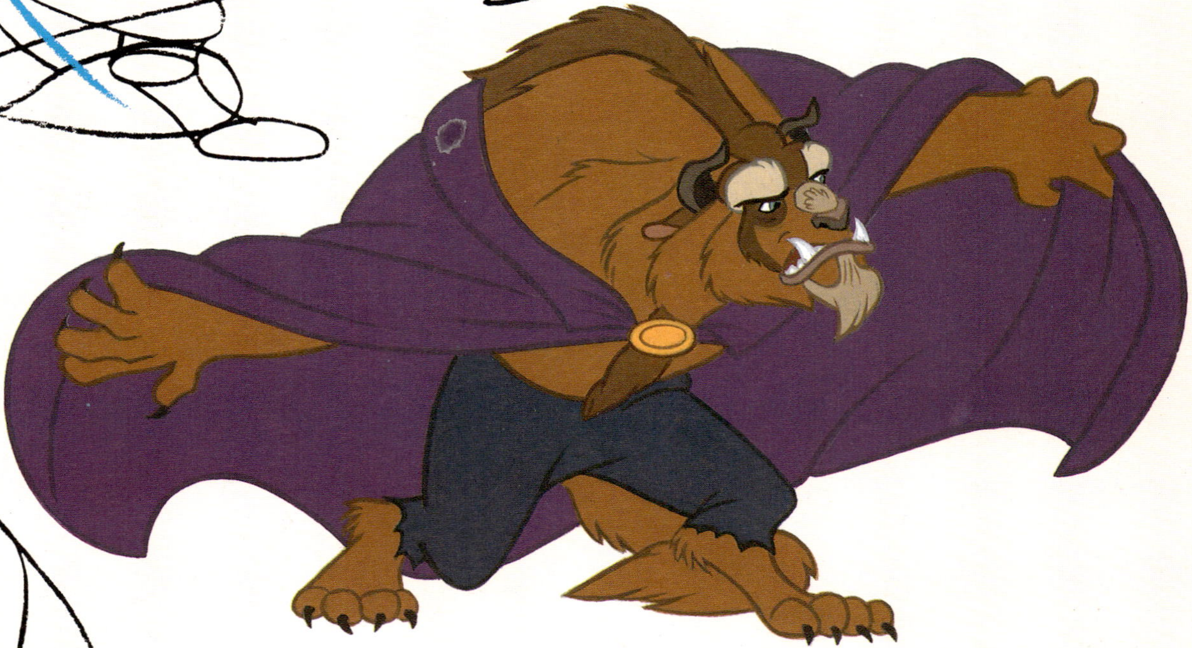

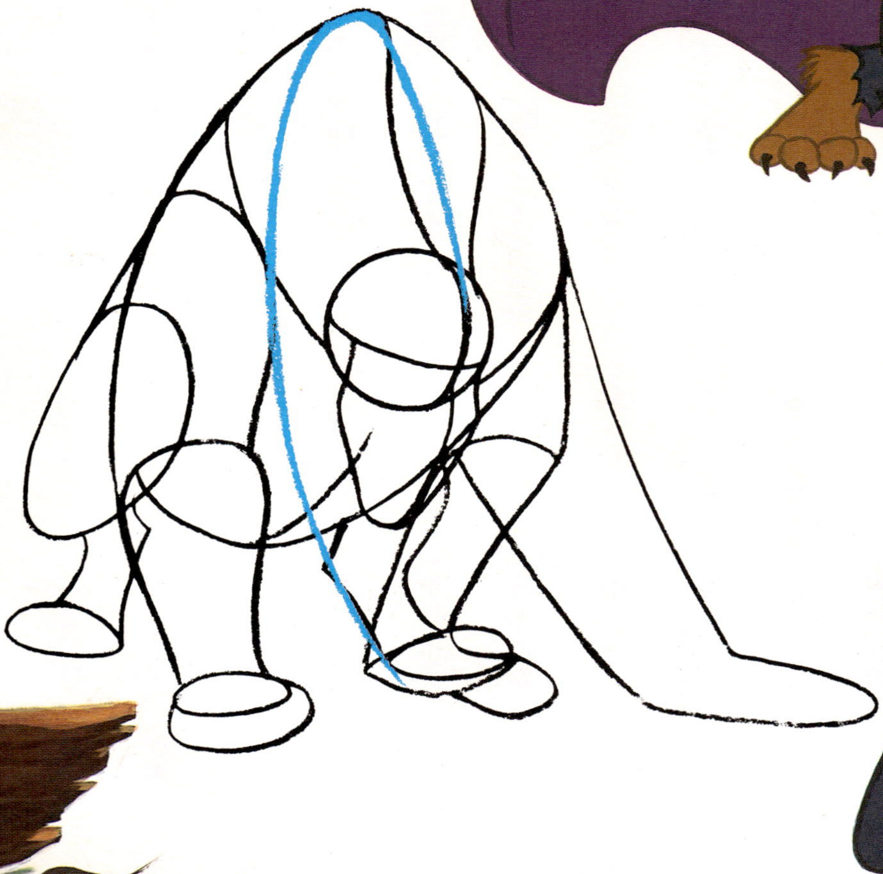

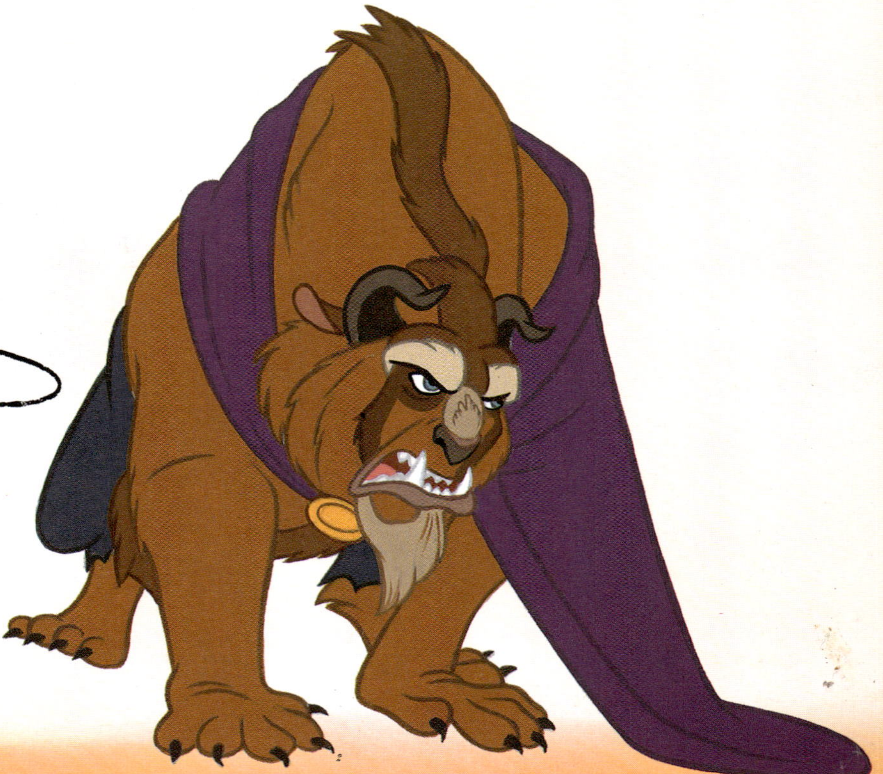

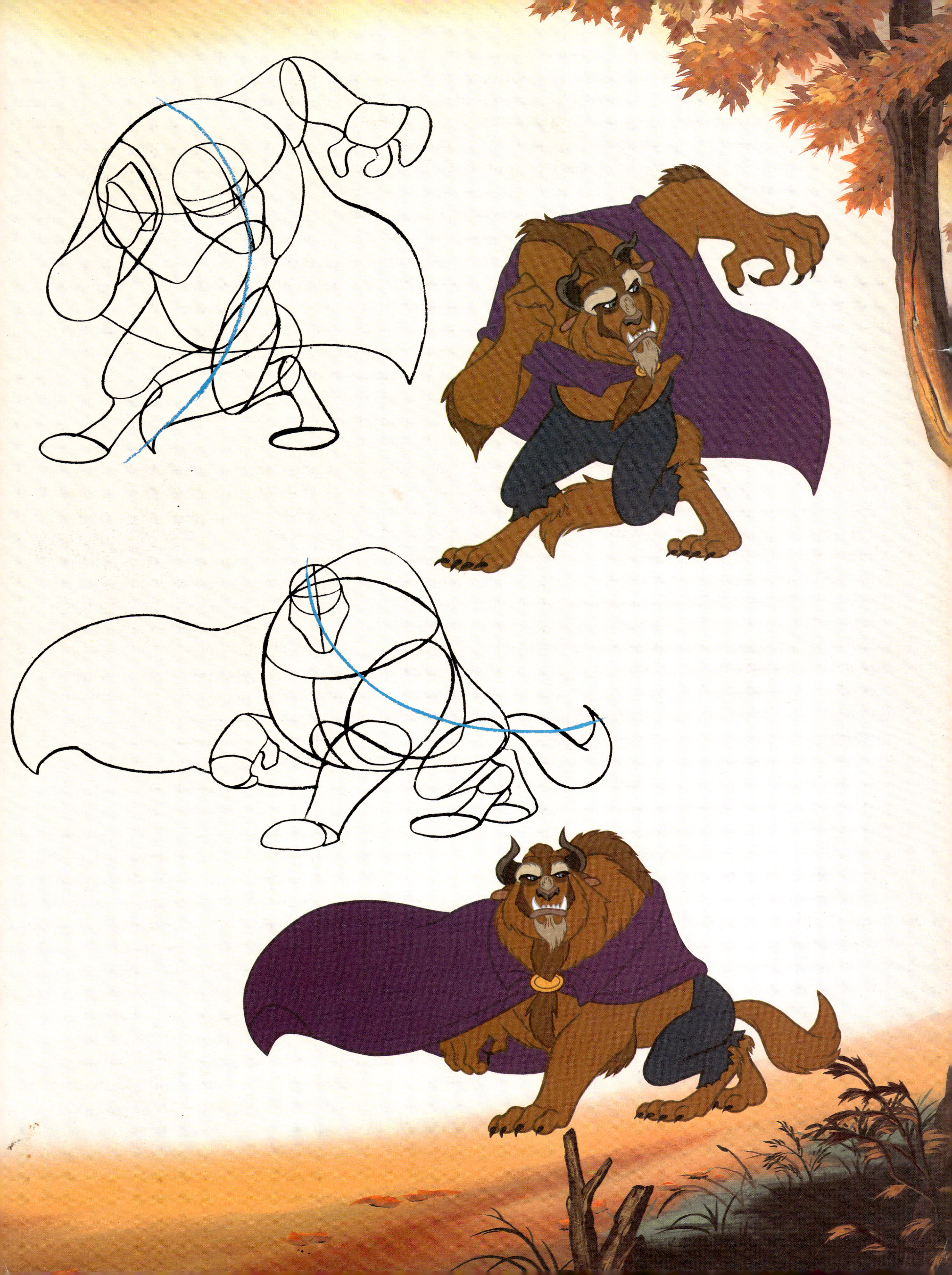

Gaston's Head

Gaston is enormously vain about his rugged good looks. Note his very strong, angular, and sharp features as you follow these steps.

1

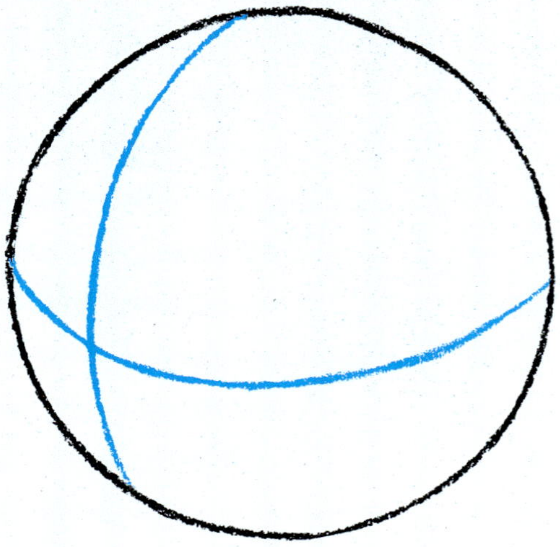

2

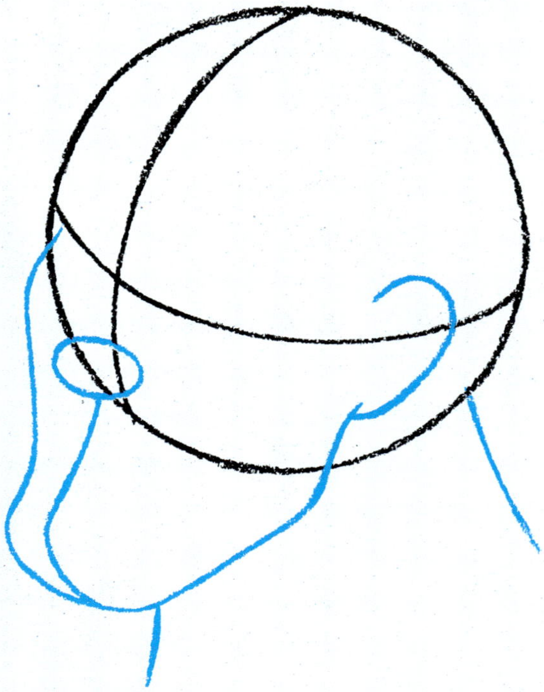

Gaston's jawline extends well below the basic ball shape of his head. Notice how his chin has a slight upward curve.

3

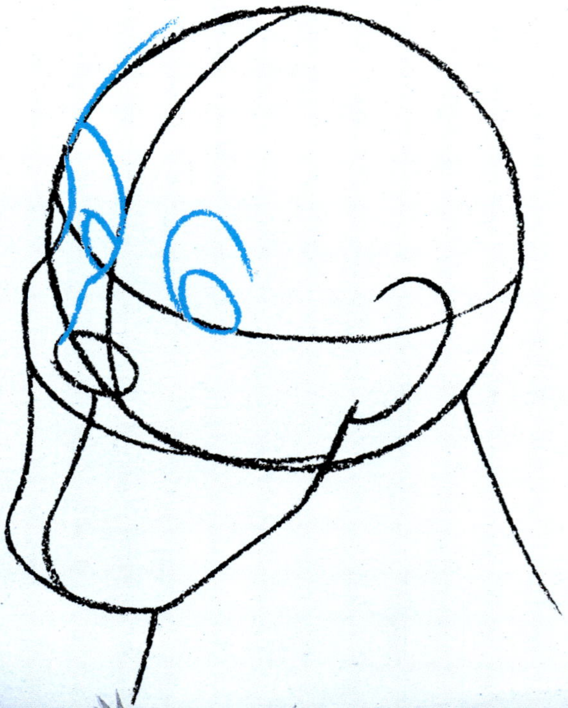

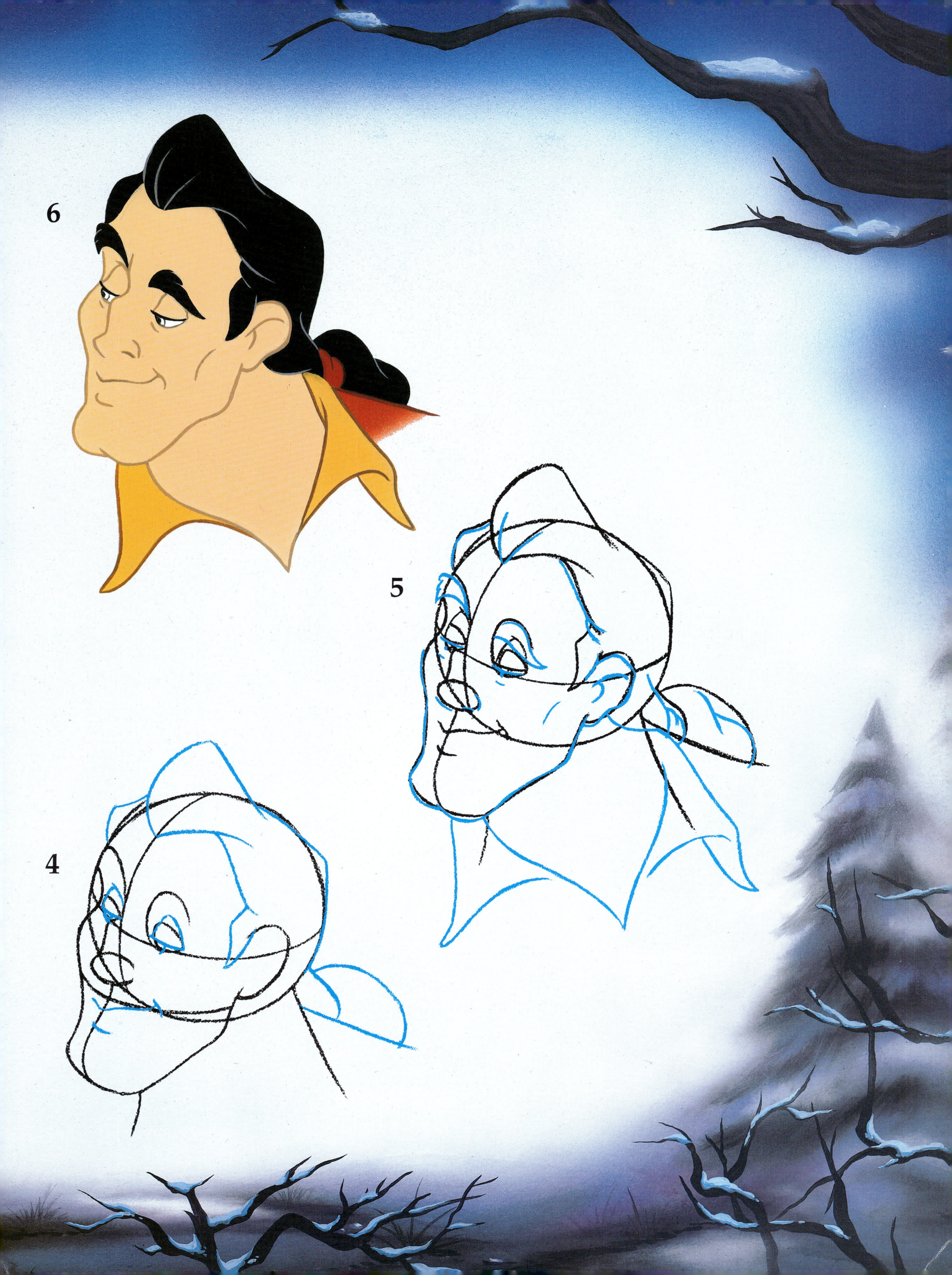
6
5
4

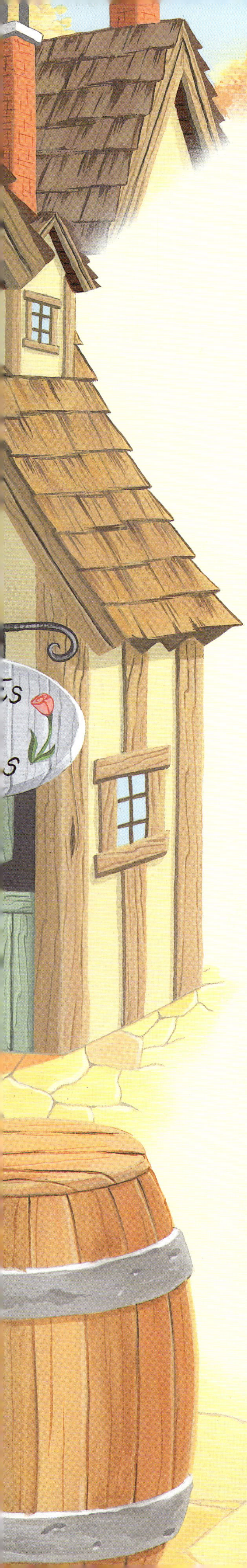

Gaston, Full Body

Gaston has the body of a weightlifter—over-developed chest and arms, narrow waist and hips, and muscular legs.

1

2

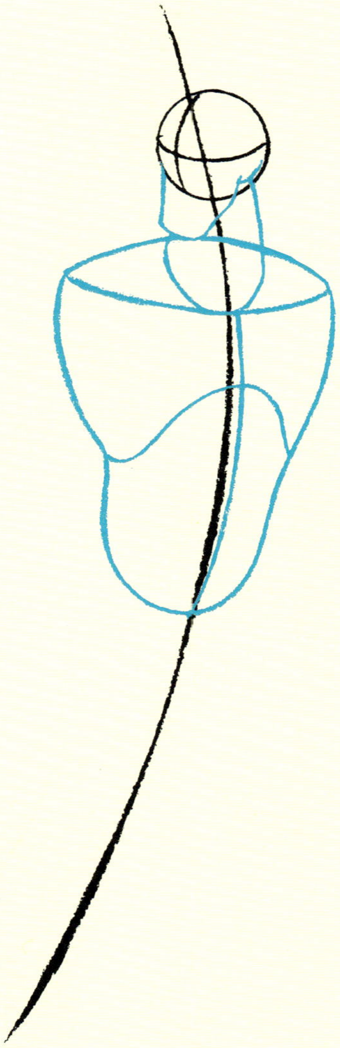

3

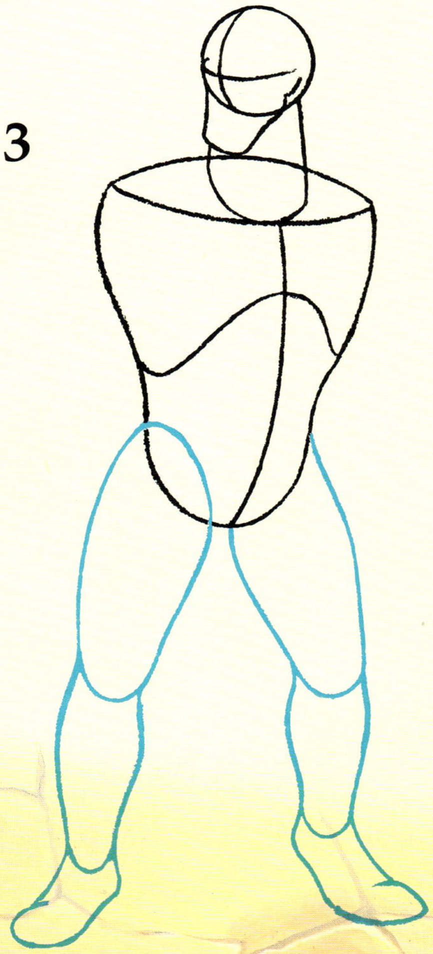

Keep Gaston's elbows slightly away from his body when his arms are down.

4

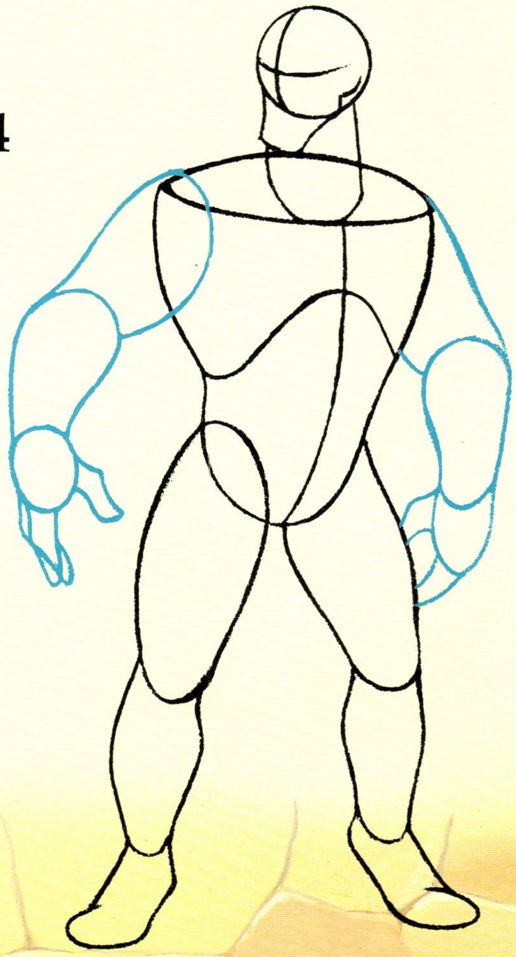

5

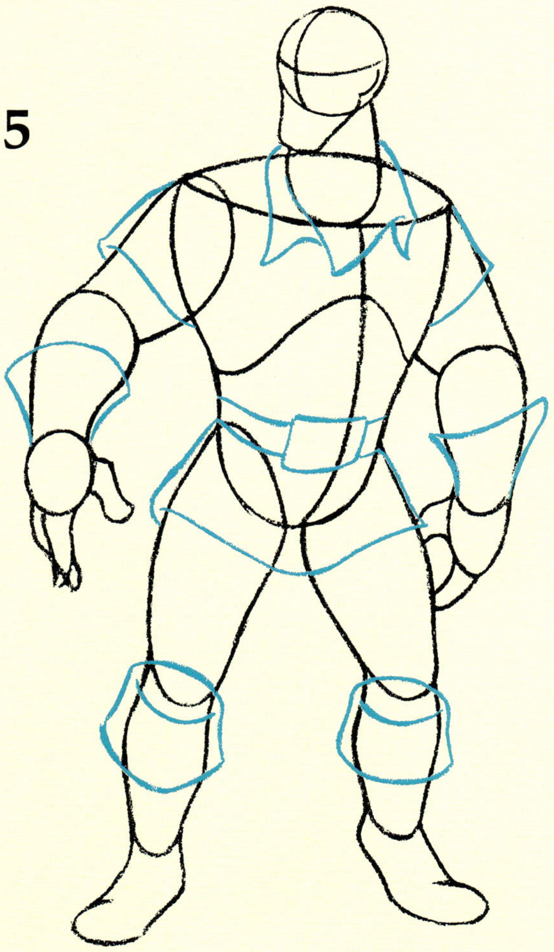

6

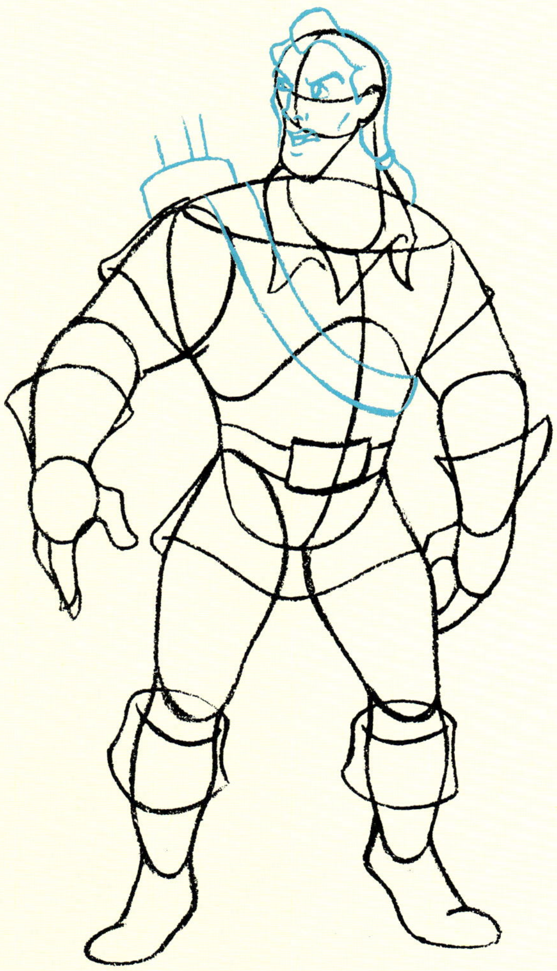

7

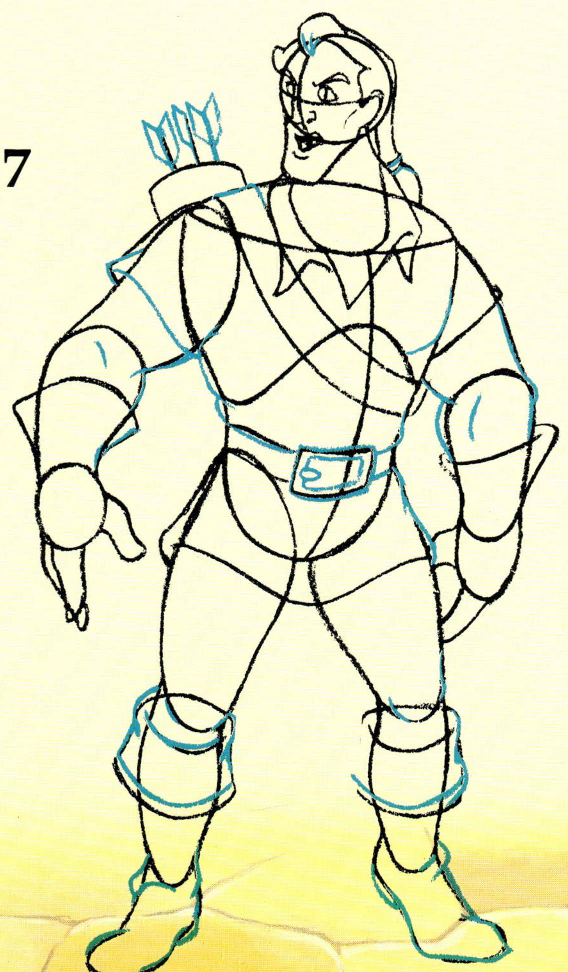

8

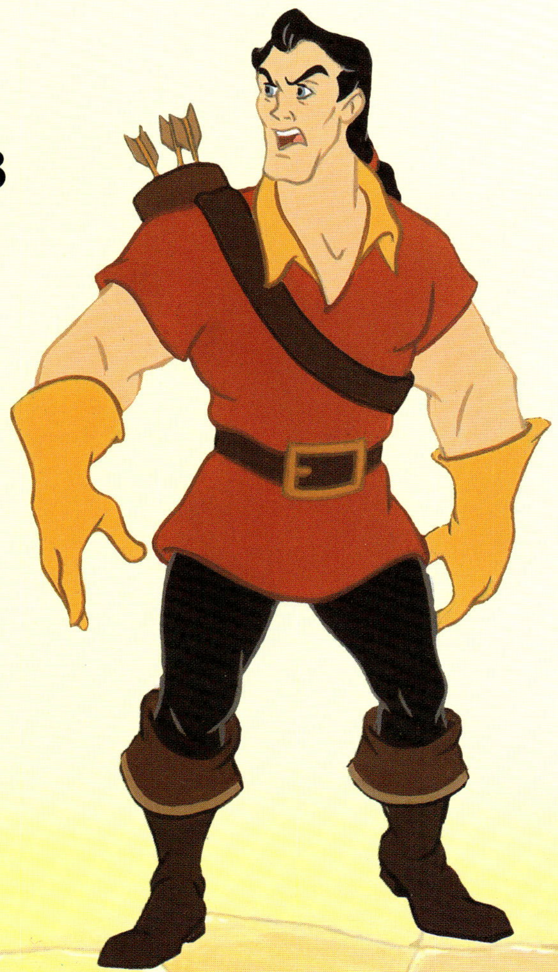

Gaston, Action Poses and Expressions

Gaston's personality can be enhanced with the right pose and expression. Practice the drawings below, then create some new ones of your own.

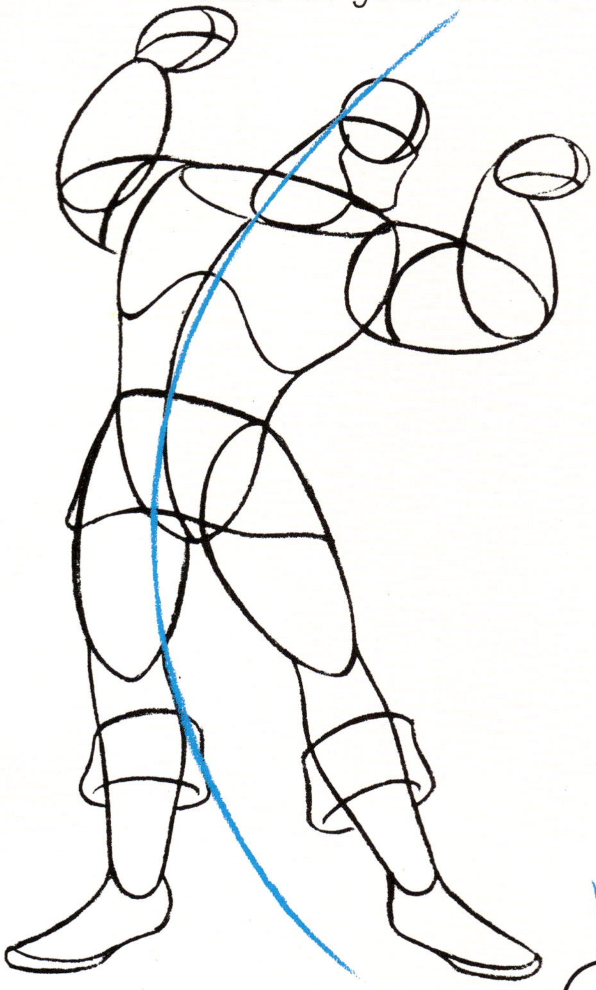

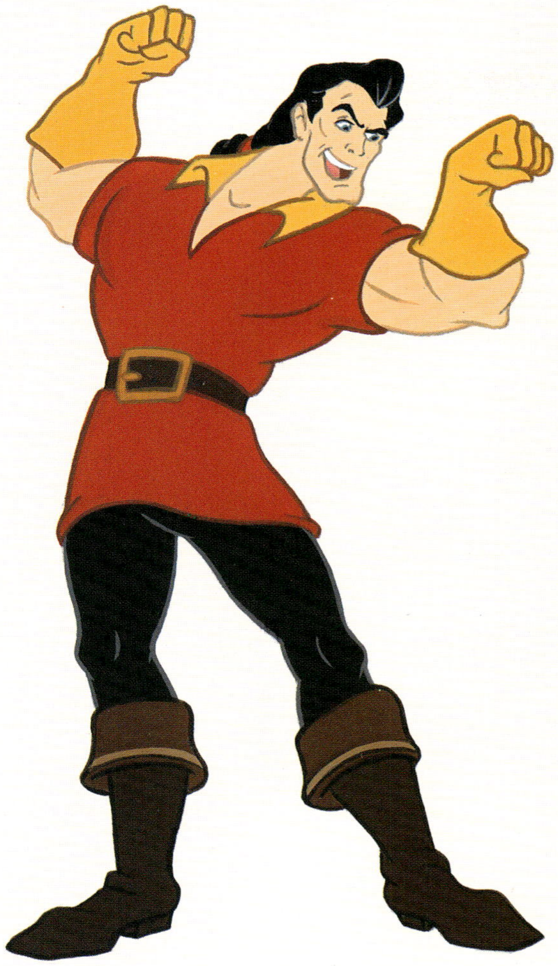

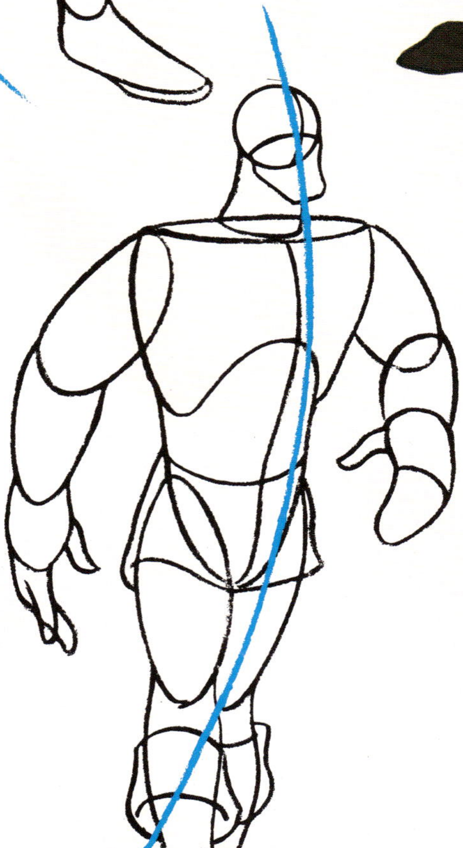

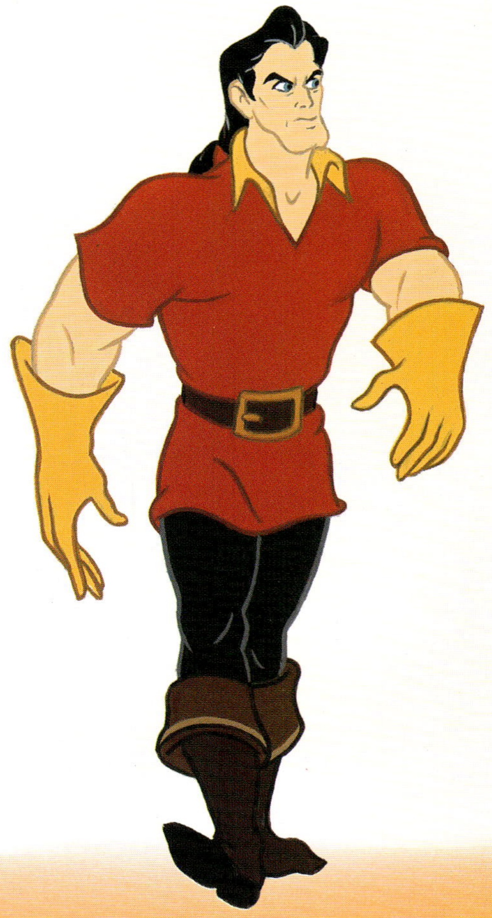

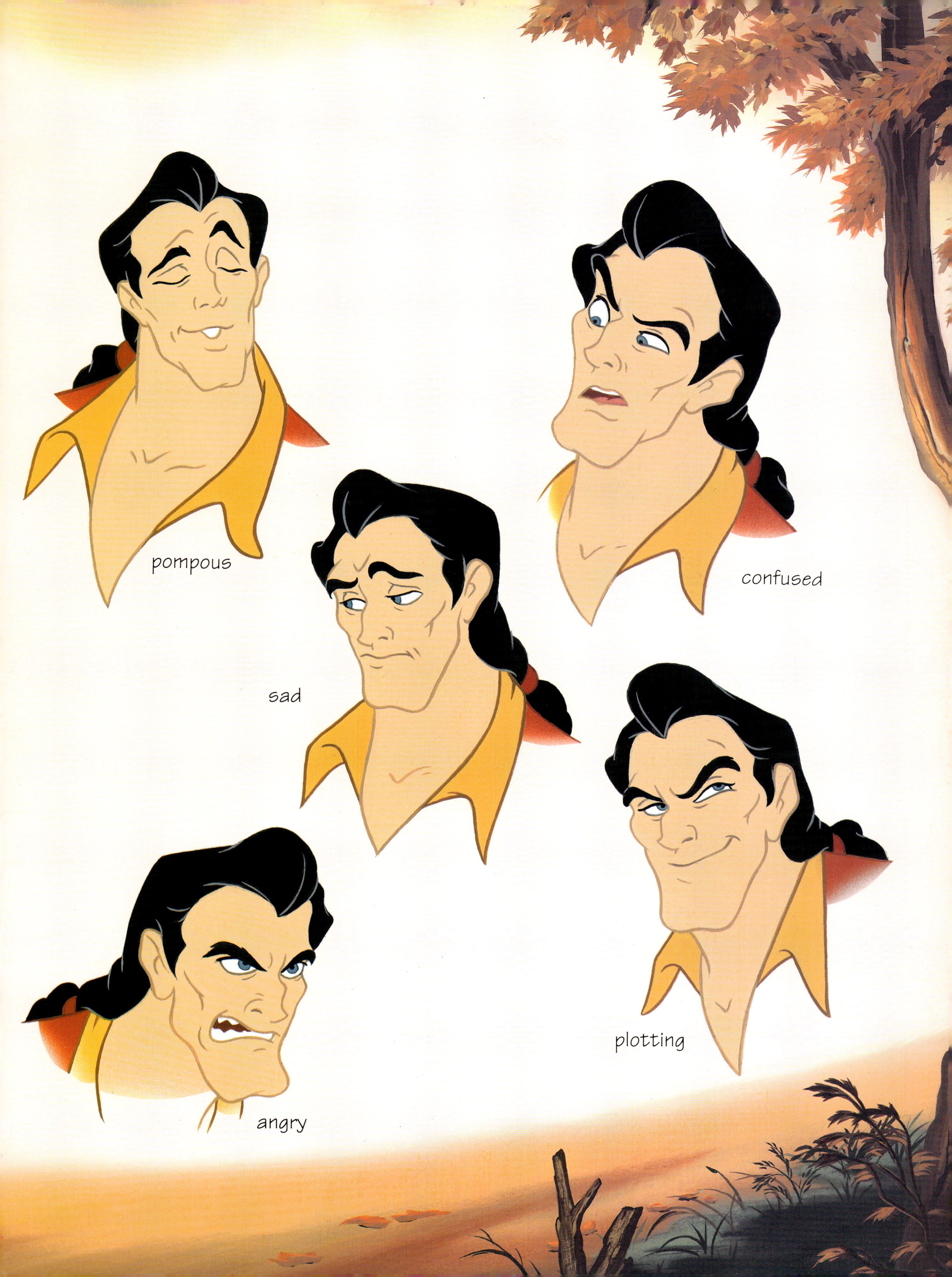
pompous
confused
sad
plotting
angry

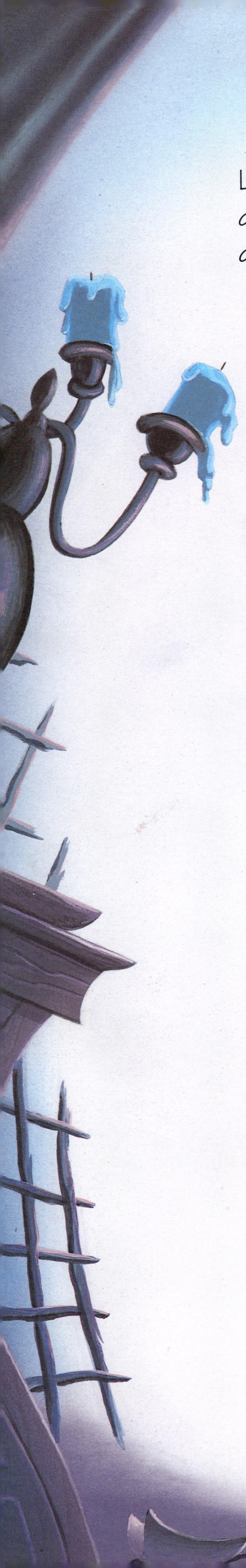

Lumiere, Full Body

Lumiere packs a lot of savoir-faire into a tiny form. The distinctive drip of wax on his forehead is an echo of a disarrayed lock of hair.

1

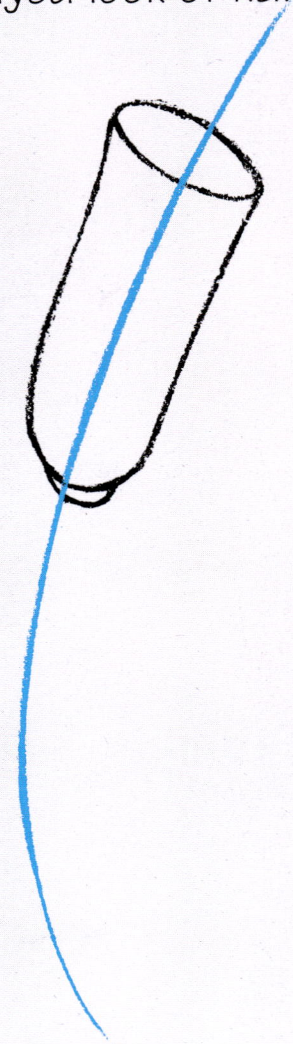

2

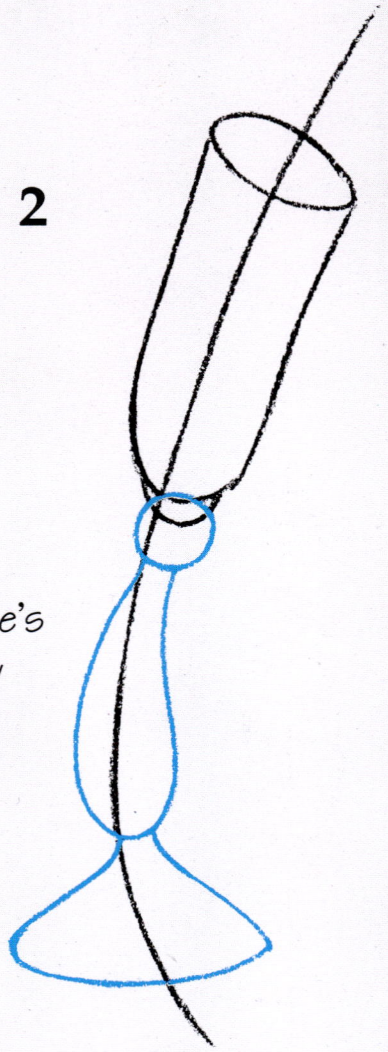

Draw Lumiere's body slightly longer than his head.

3

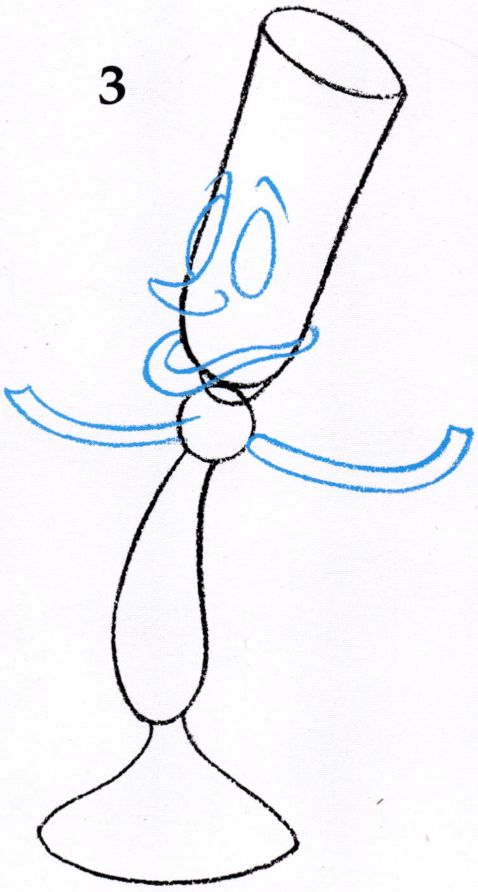

Notice how his head slightly tapers to the base.

4

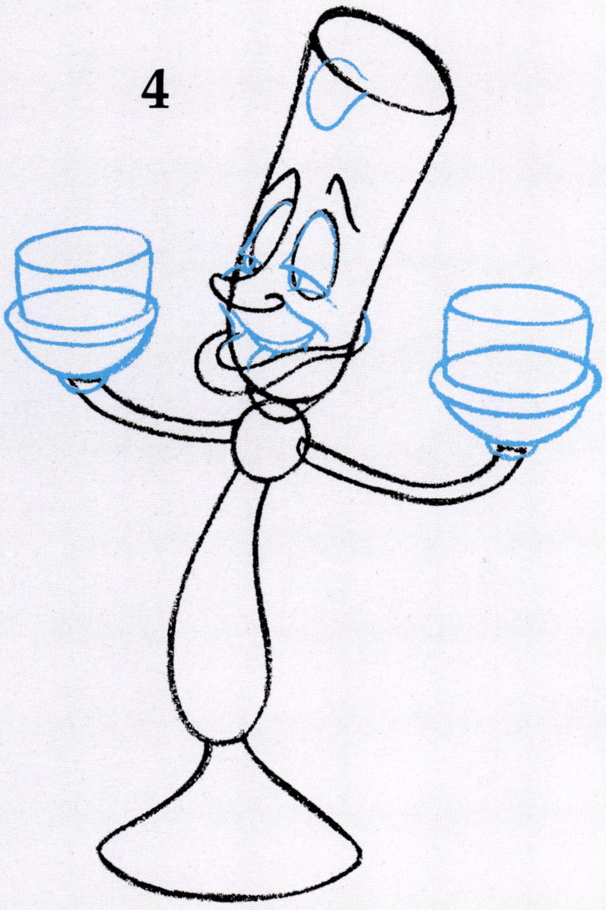

5

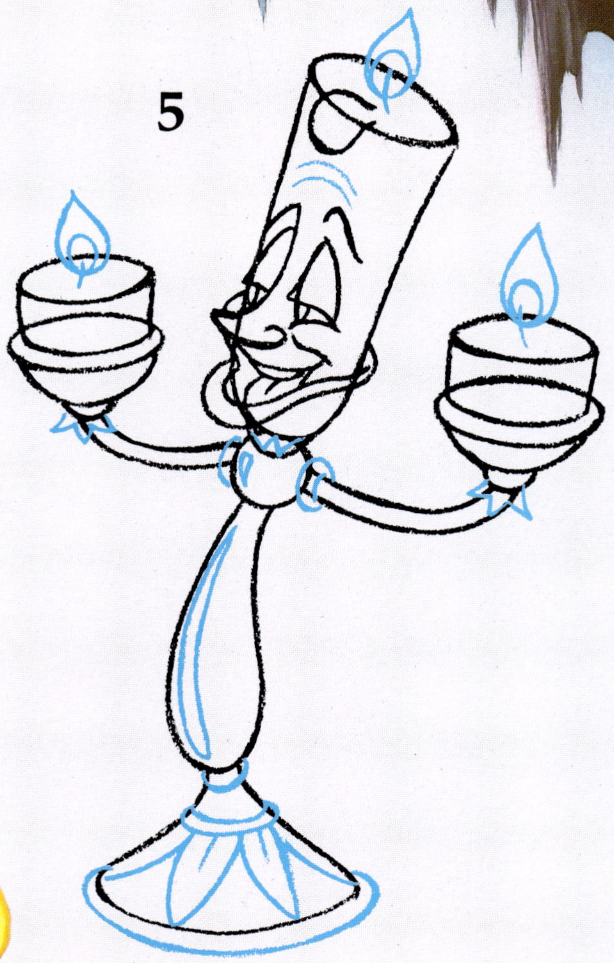

6

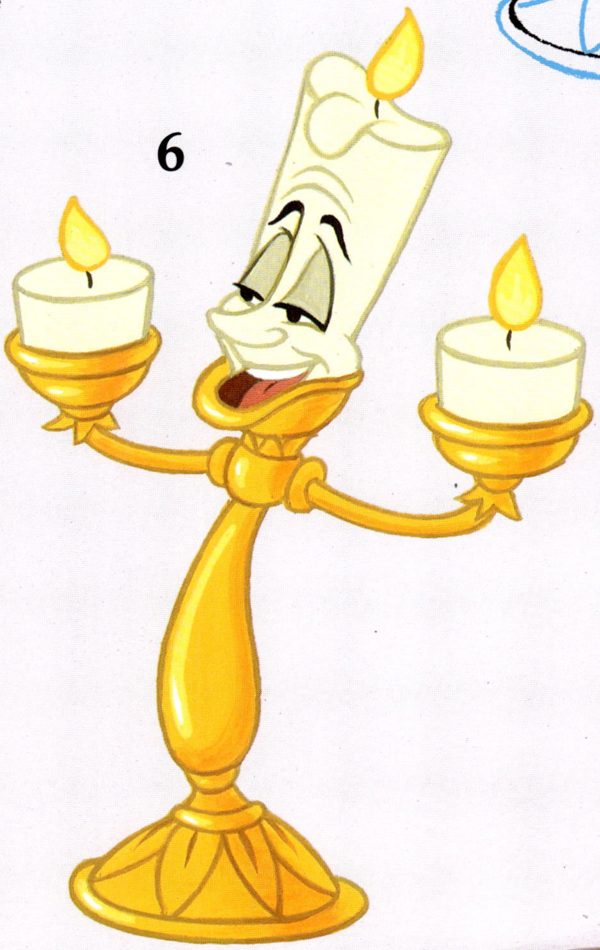

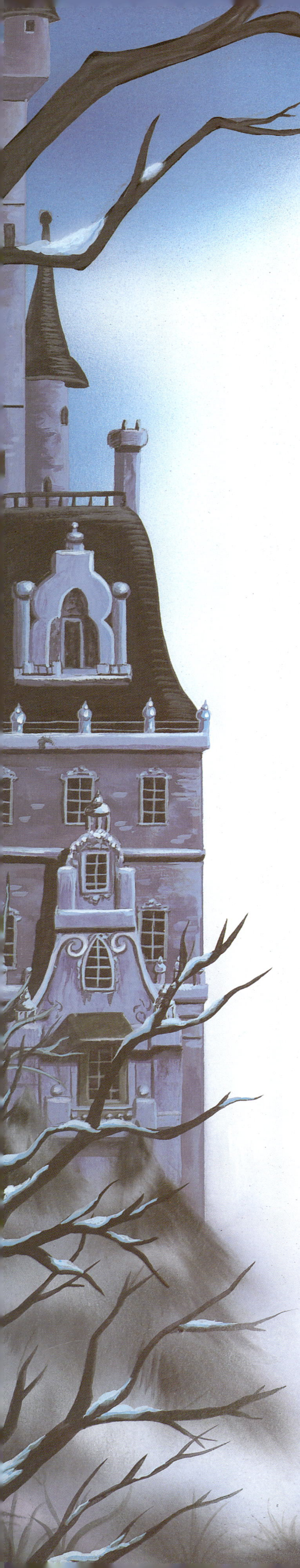

Cogsworth, Full Body

Cogsworth is a stuffy and serious mantle clock. Although he does not wear clothes, the details on his body give the look of a uniform.

1

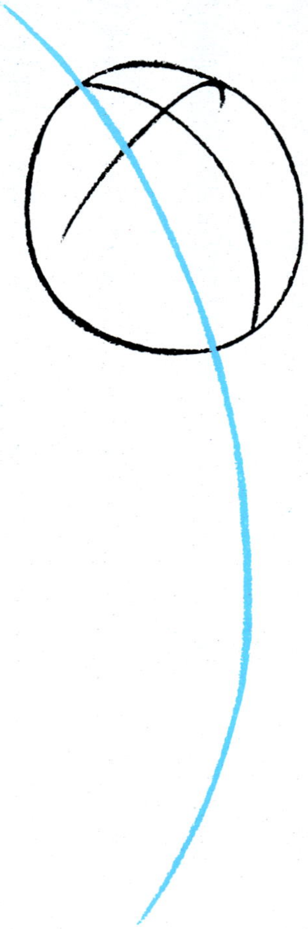

2

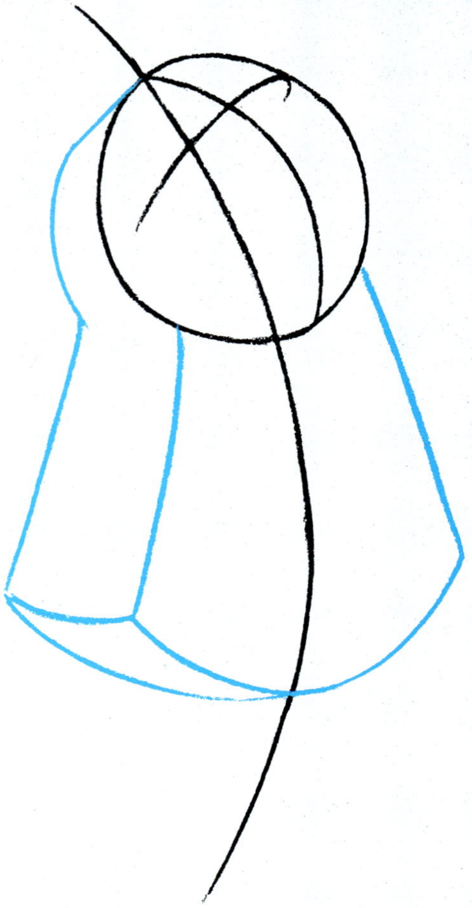

5

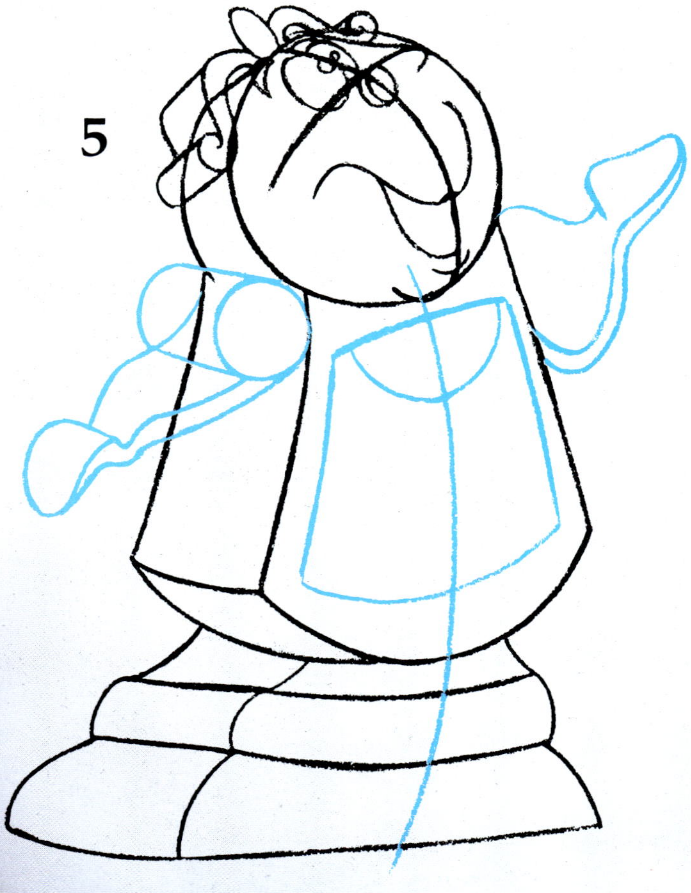

6

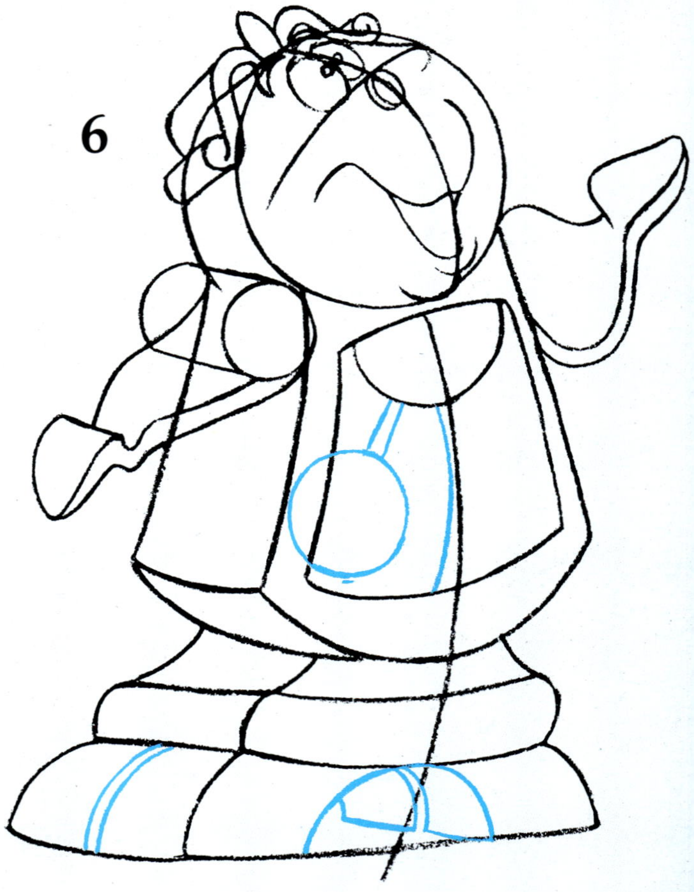

3

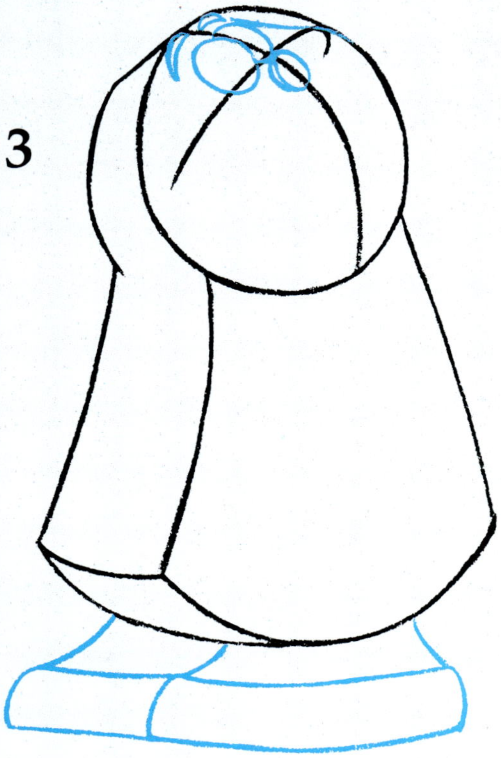

4

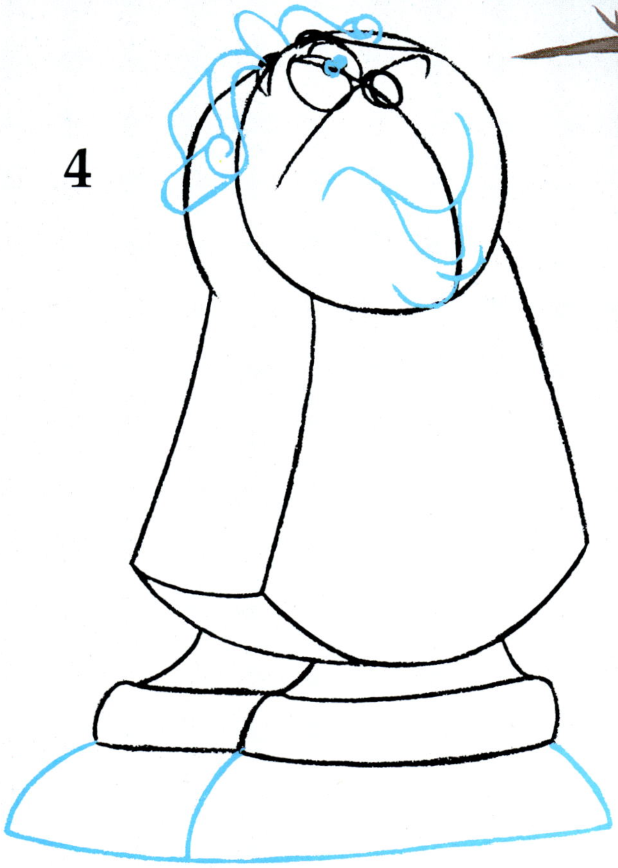

7

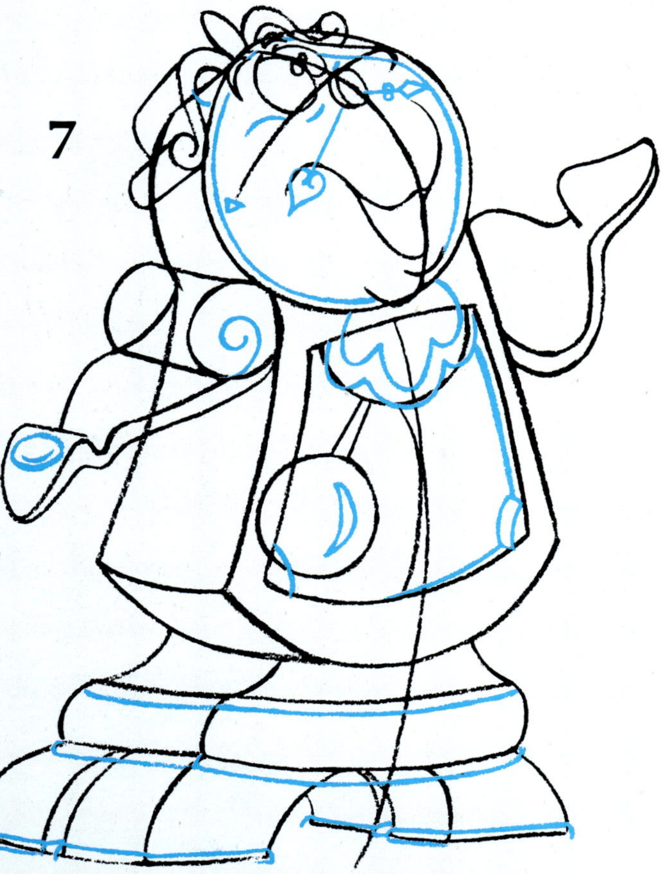

8

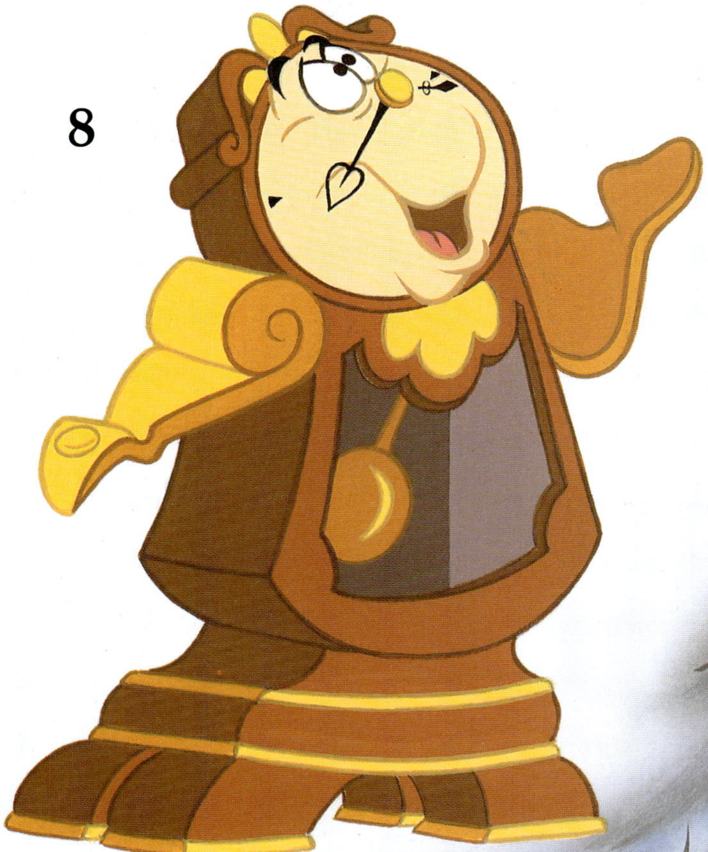

Mrs. Potts and Chip, Full Body

Mrs. Potts and her son Chip are cheerful and lively, despite being pieces of china.

3

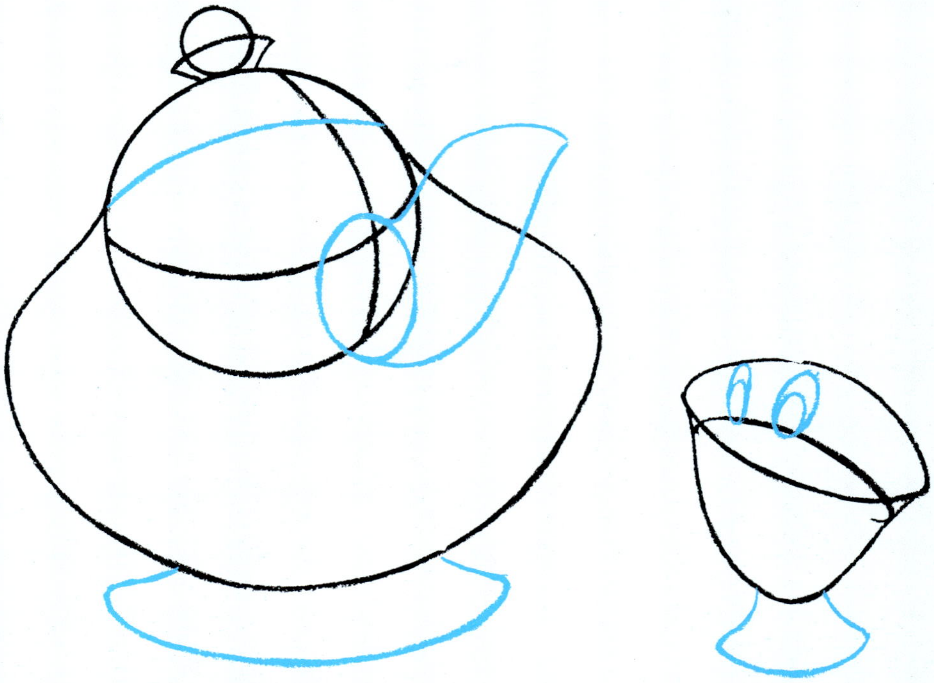

2

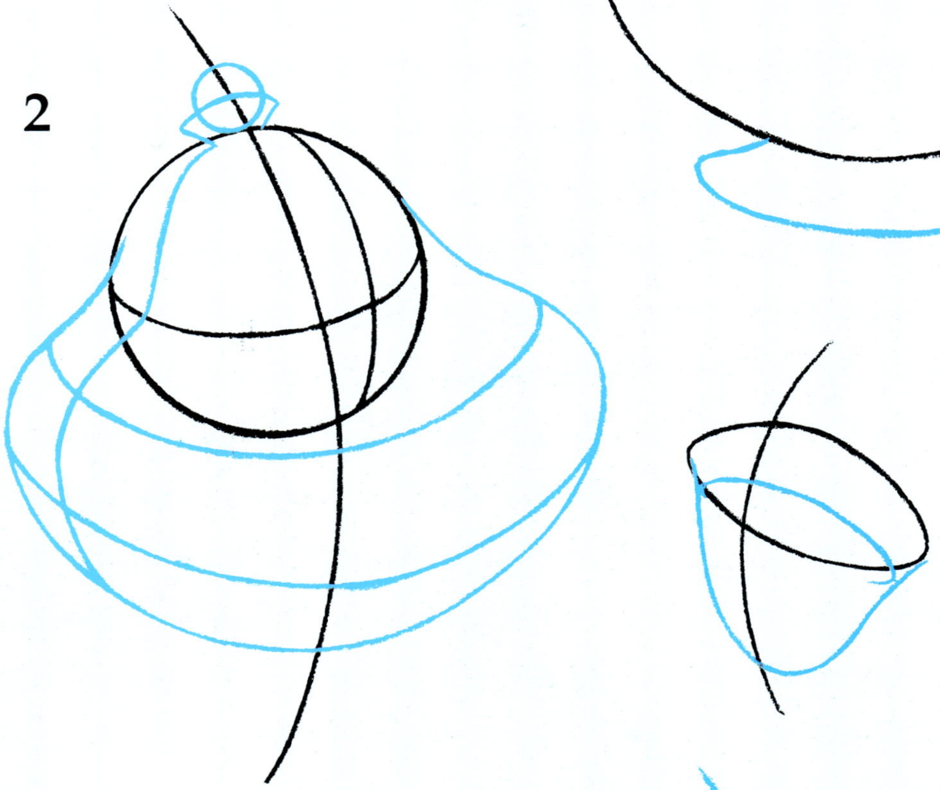

Draw a squat pear shape for Mrs. Potts's body.

1

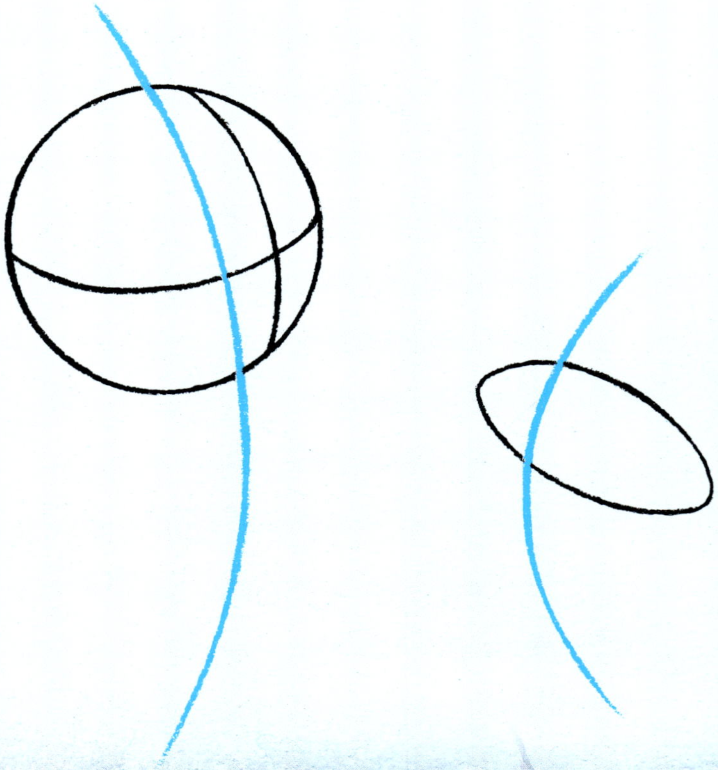

4

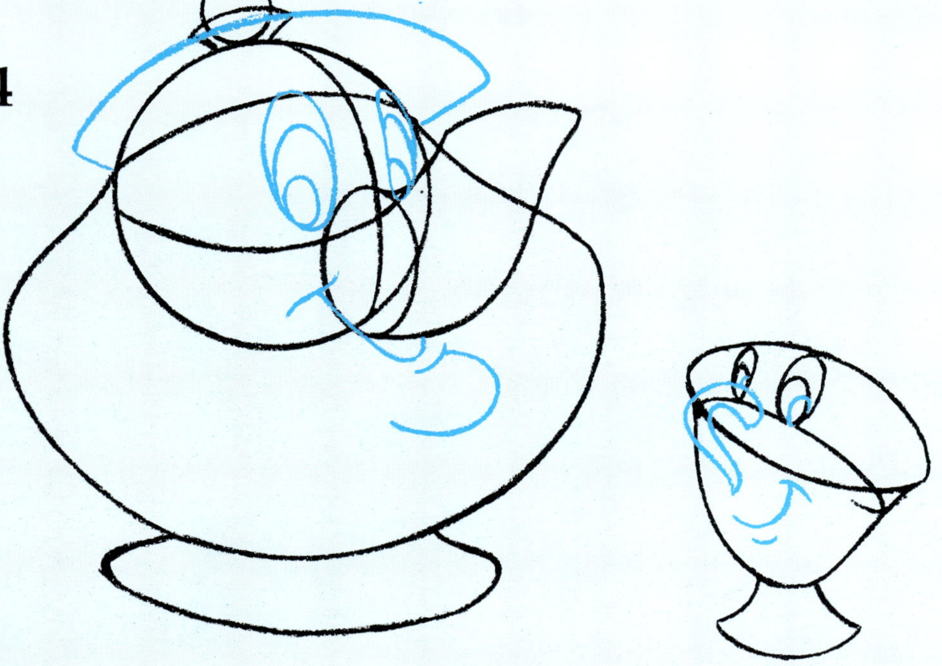

5

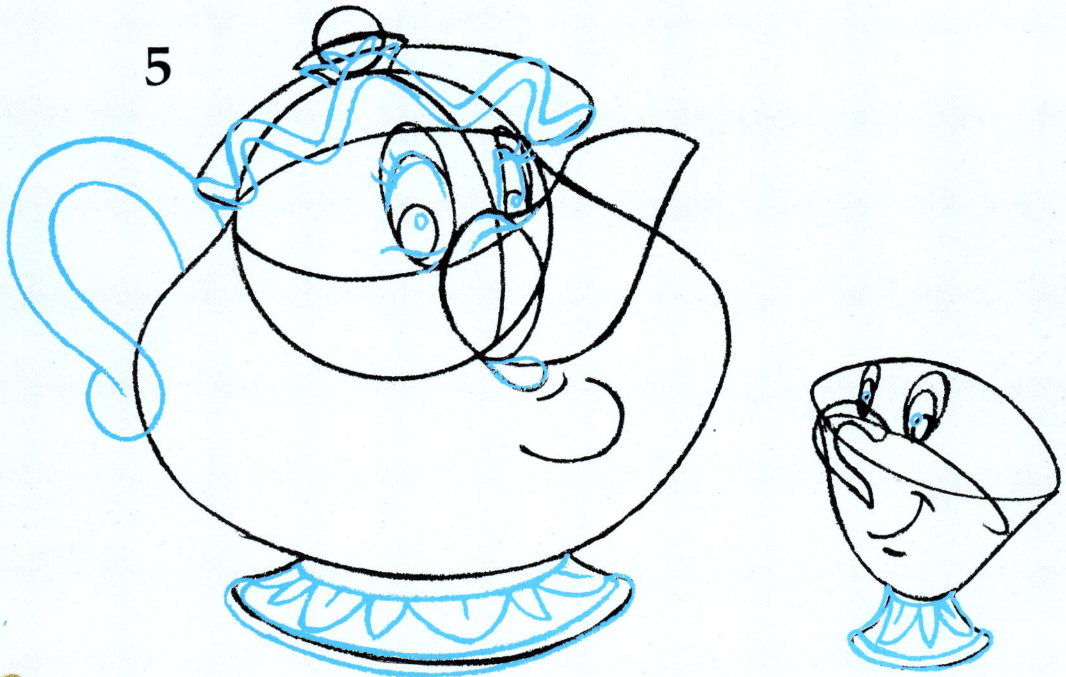

6

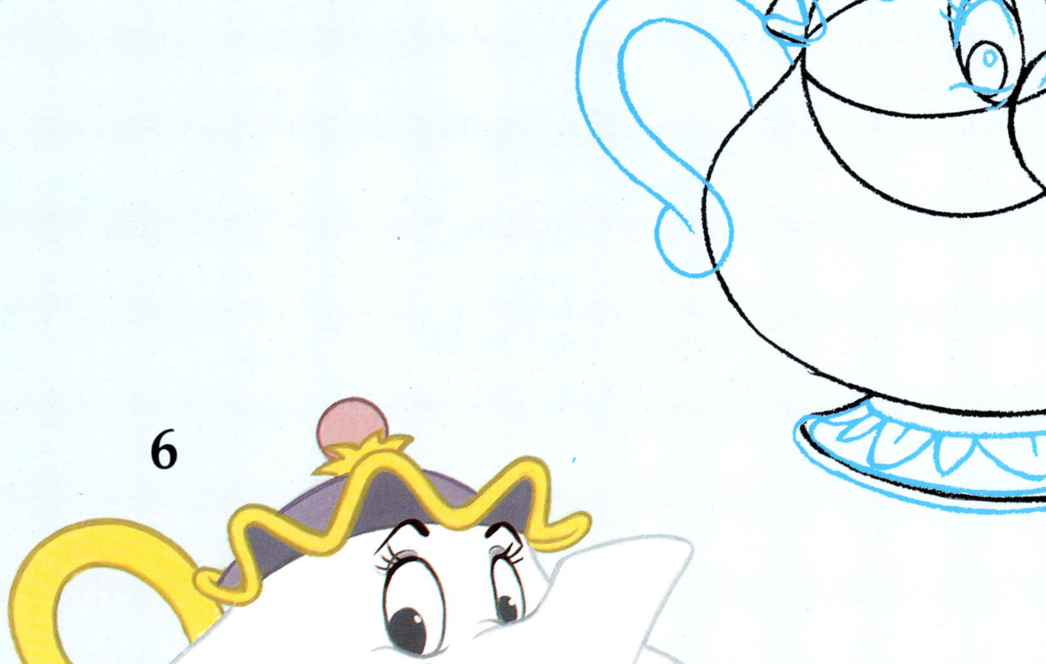

Lumiere and Cogsworth, Action Poses

Lumiere and Cogsworth have unusual bodies, but they manage to move in a very human fashion. Notice how they use their parts like arms and legs.

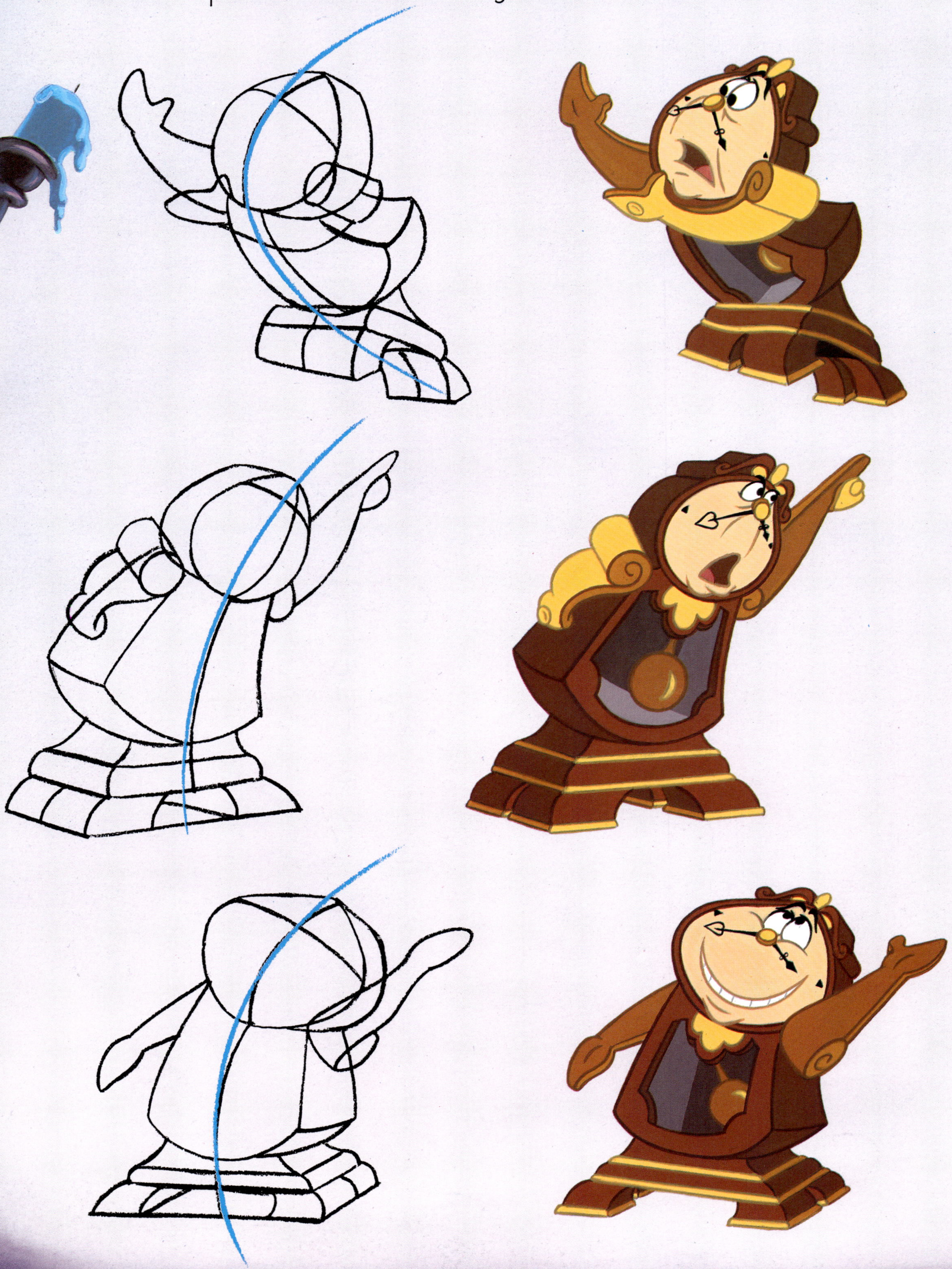

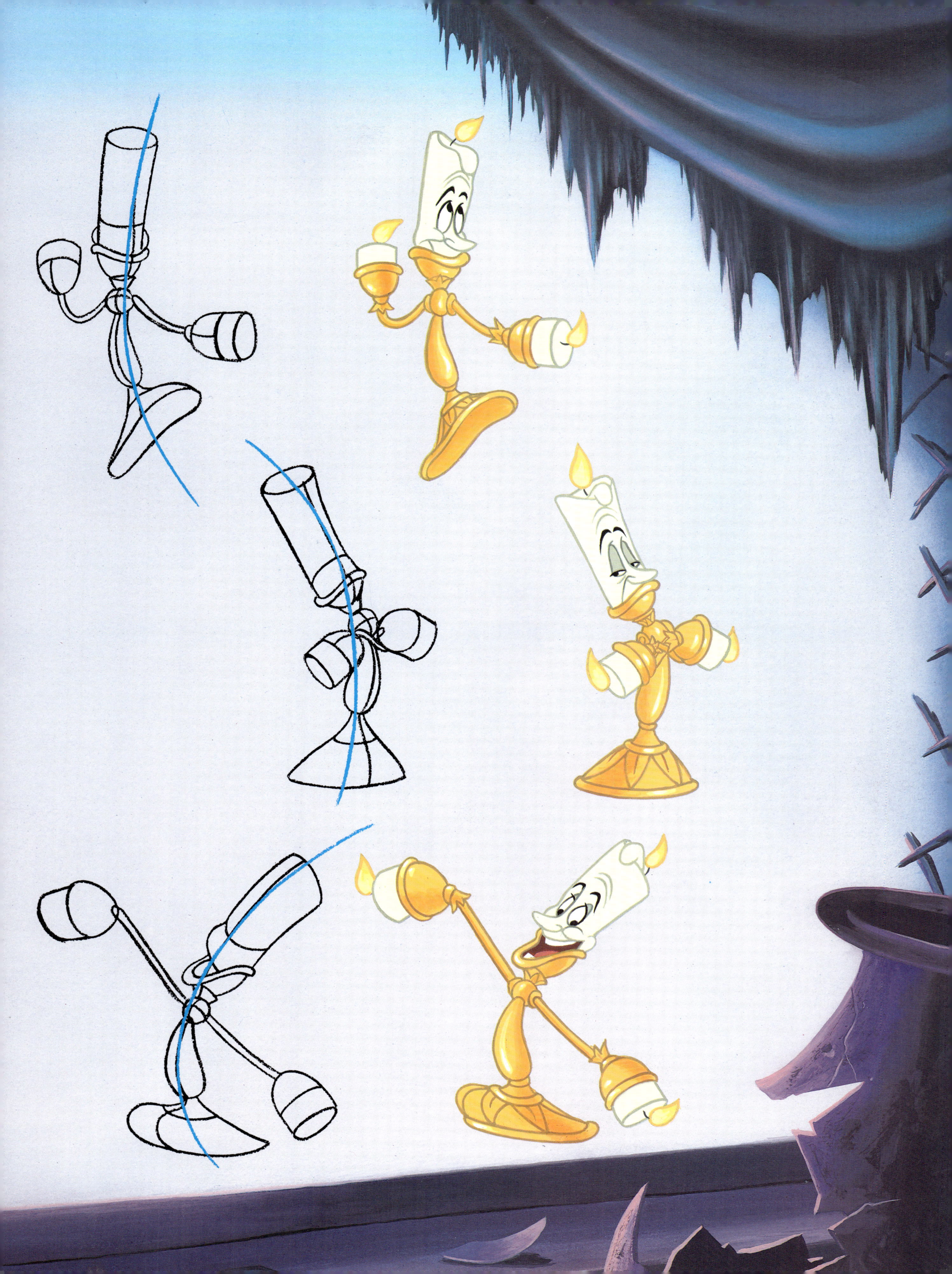

Mrs. Potts and Chip, Action Poses

Mrs. Potts is a warmhearted teapot. Chip, a teacup, is like a wide-eyed child. Keep these traits in mind as you draw them in these action poses.

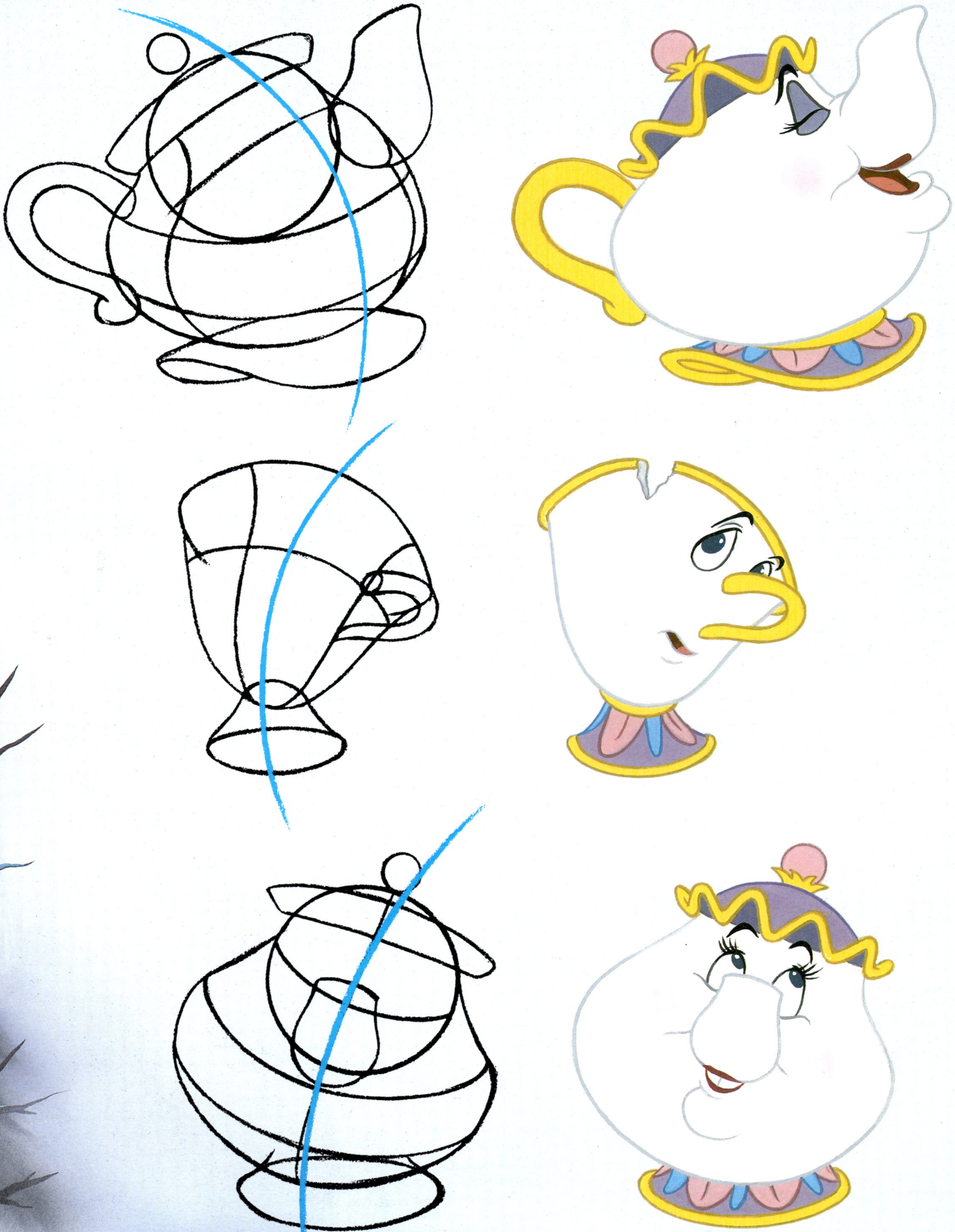

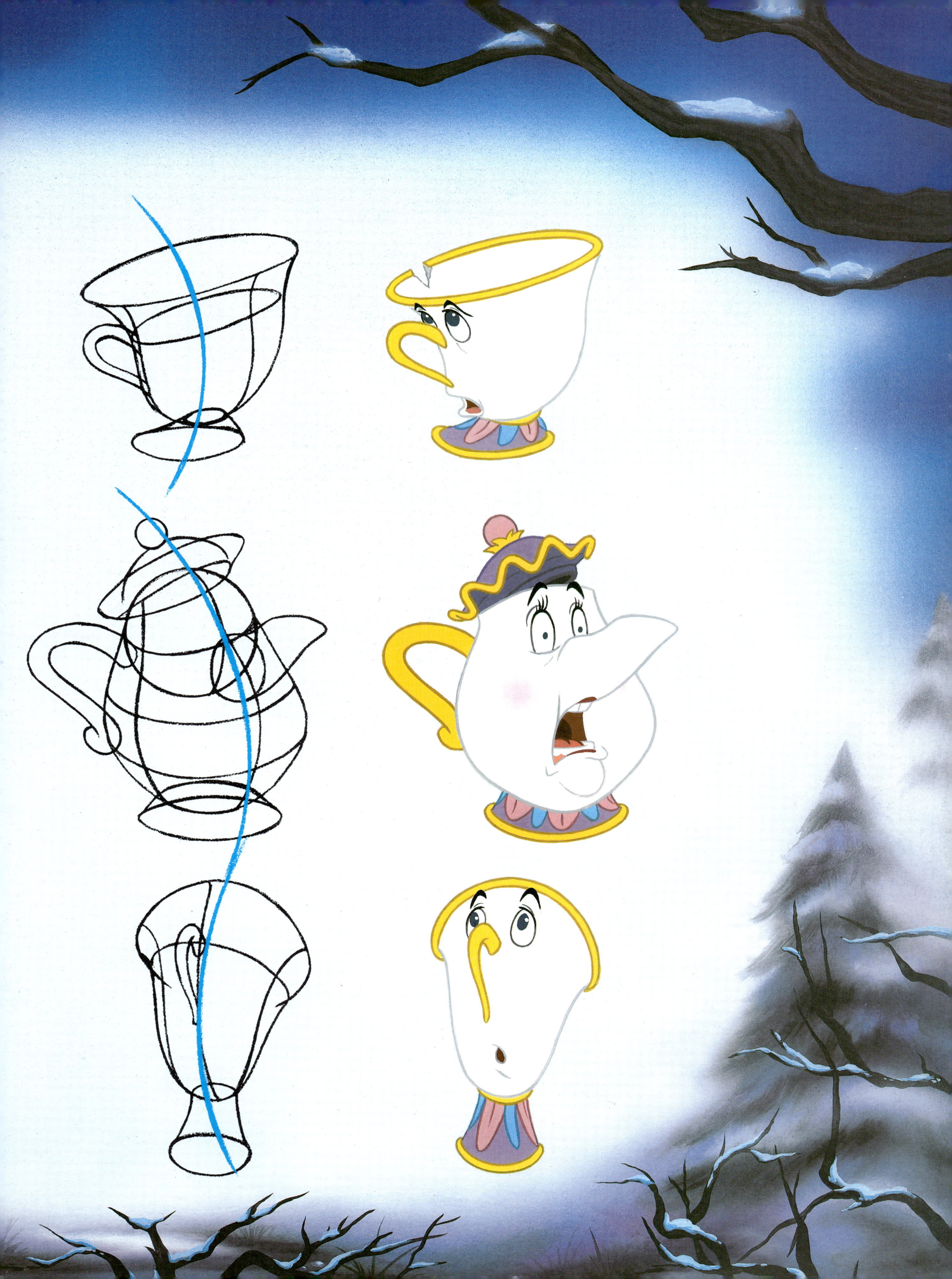

More Costumes and Characters

After you have practiced drawing the Beast and Belle, try putting them in formal wear. Then try drawing the rest of the *Beauty and the Beast* cast.

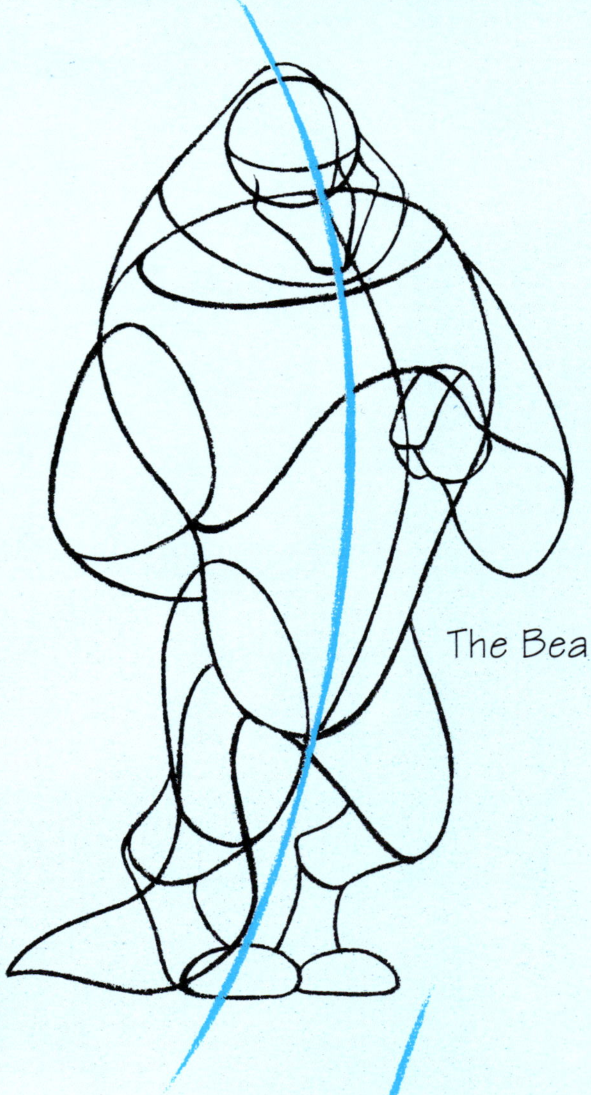

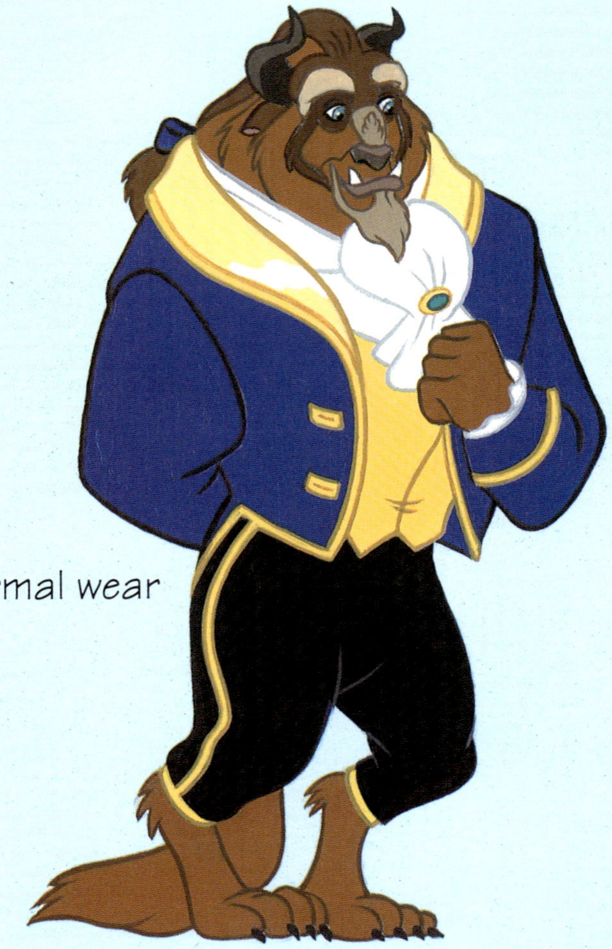

The Beast in formal wear

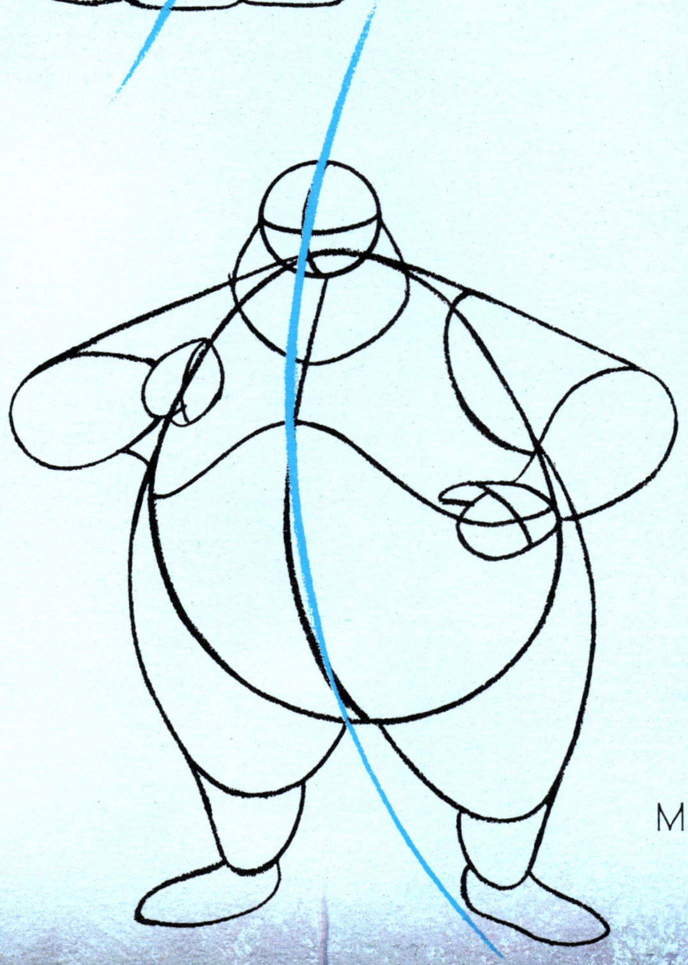

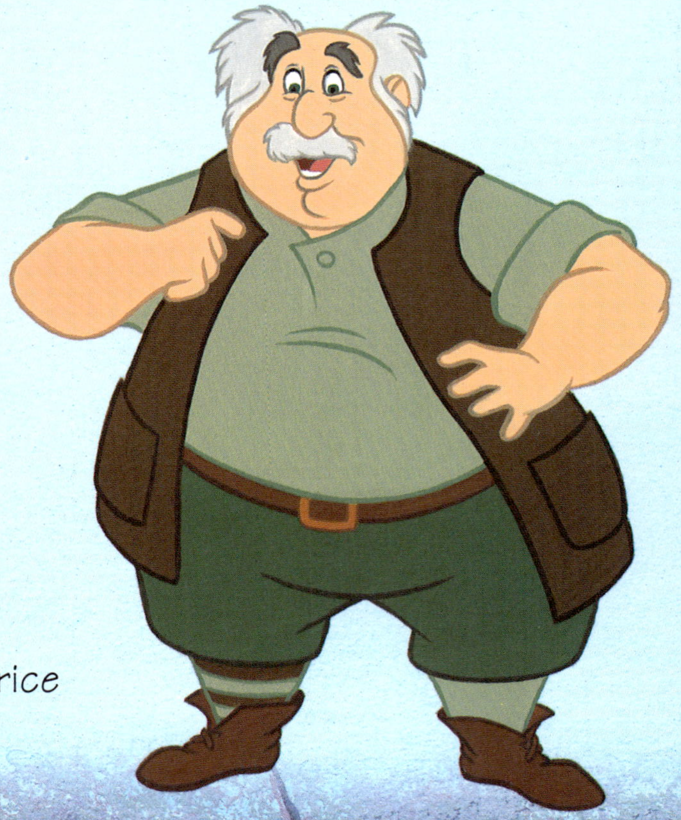

Maurice

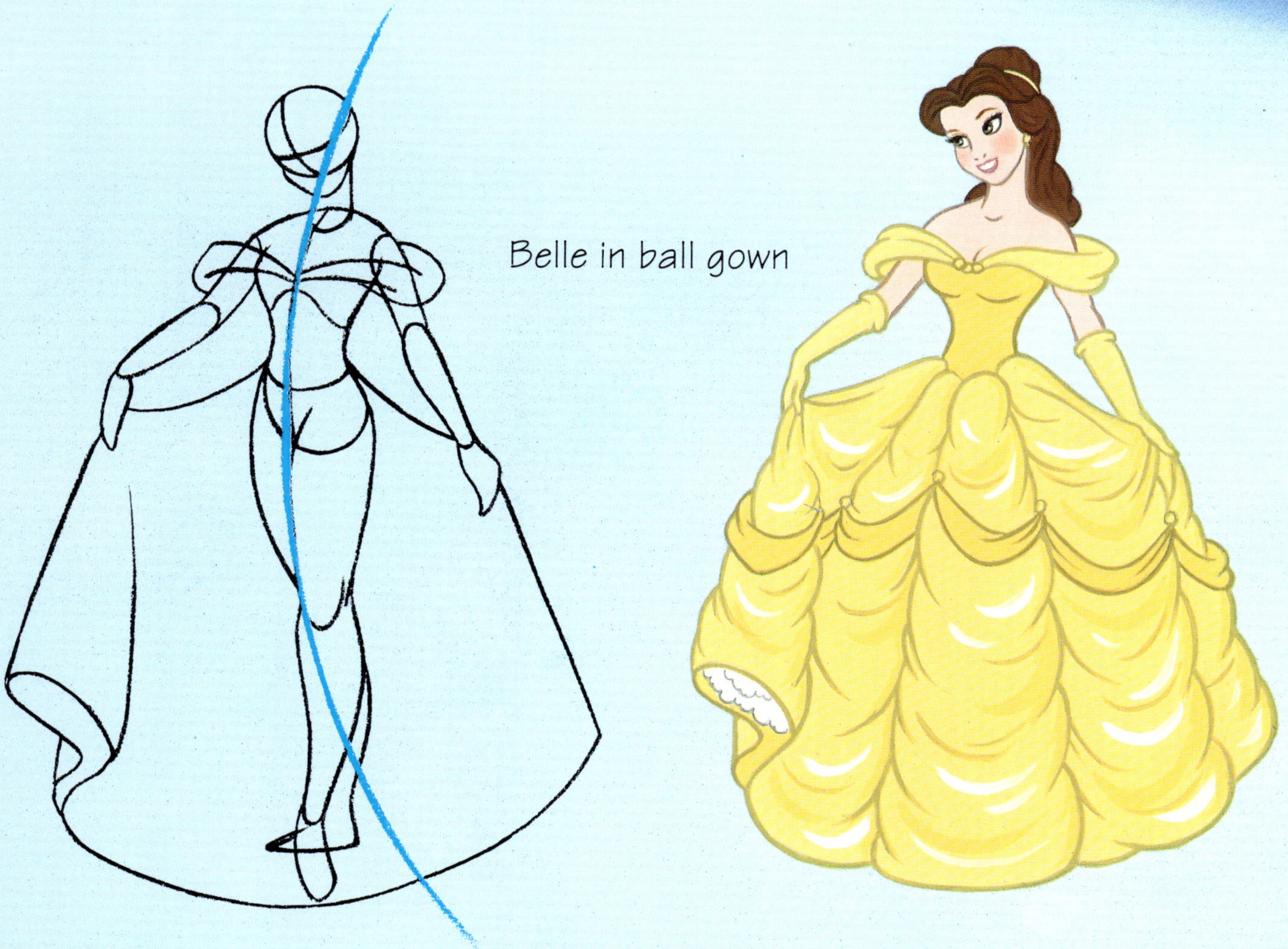

Belle in ball gown

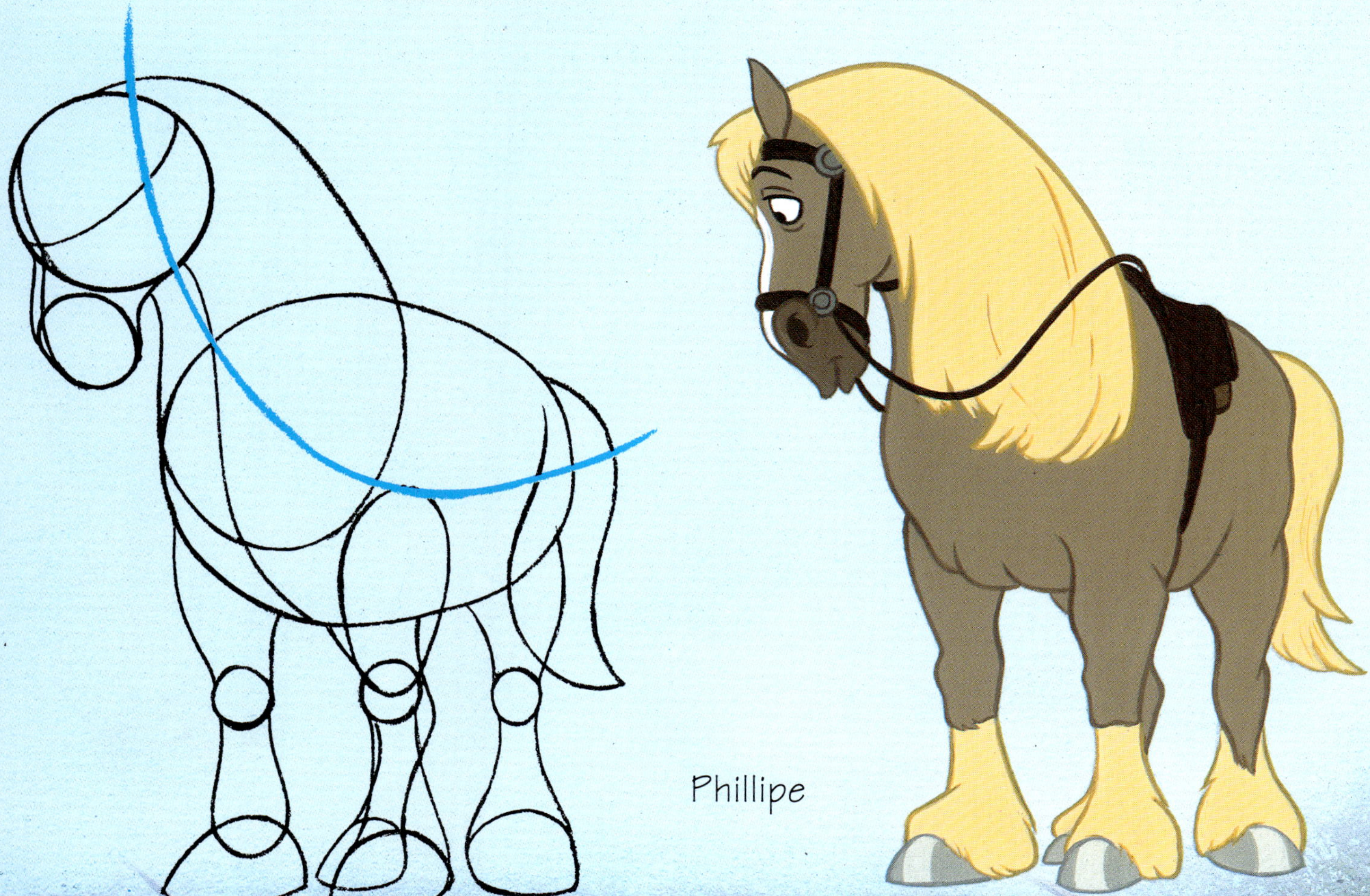

Phillipe

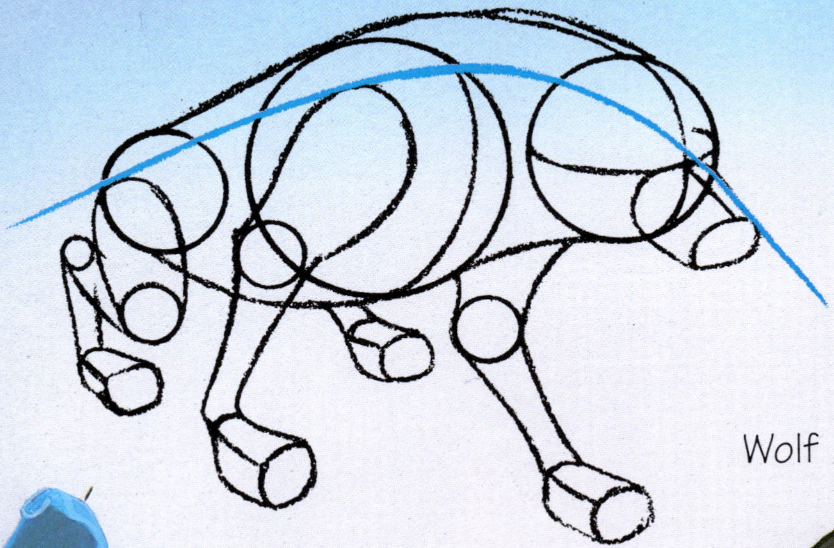

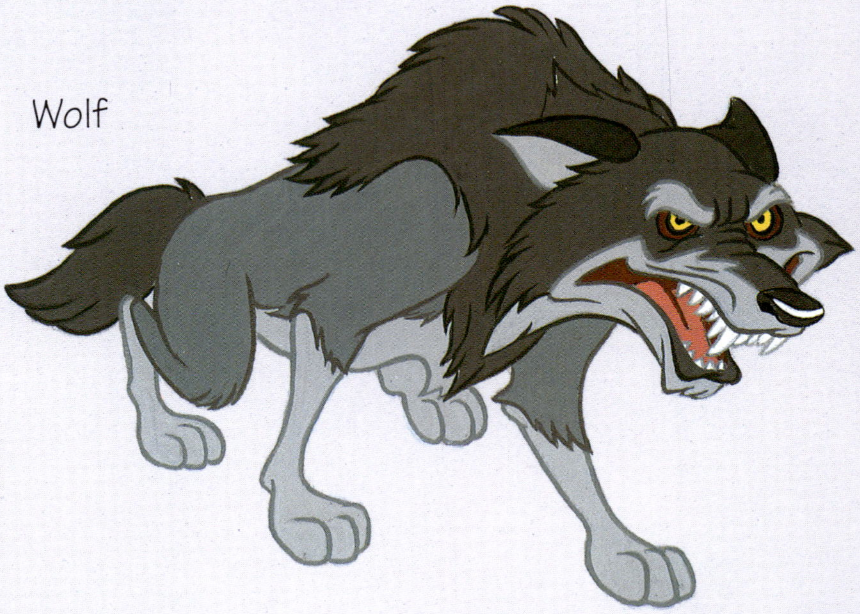

Wolf

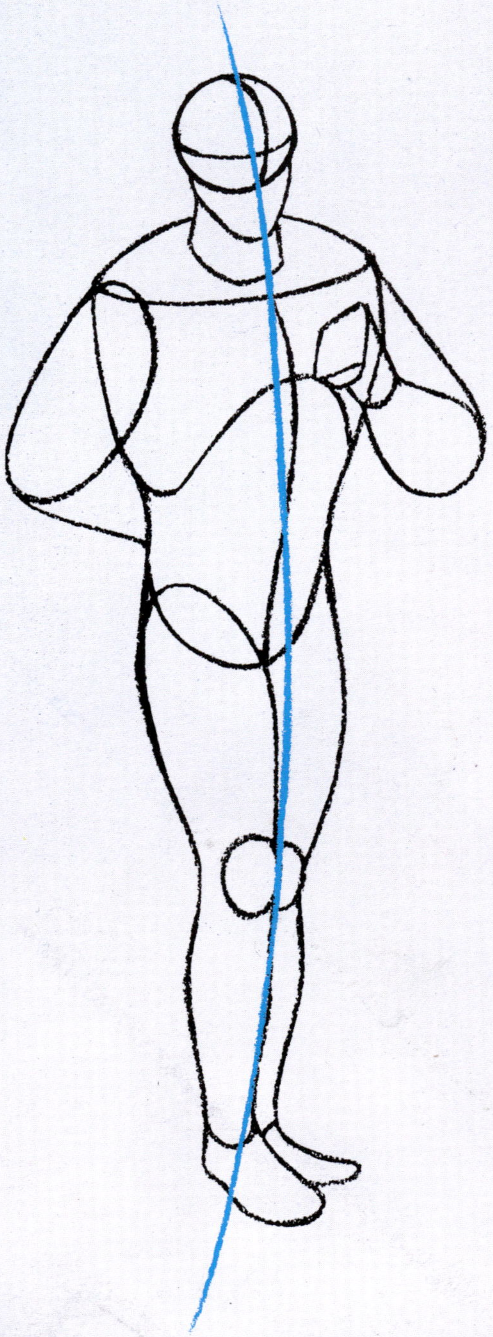

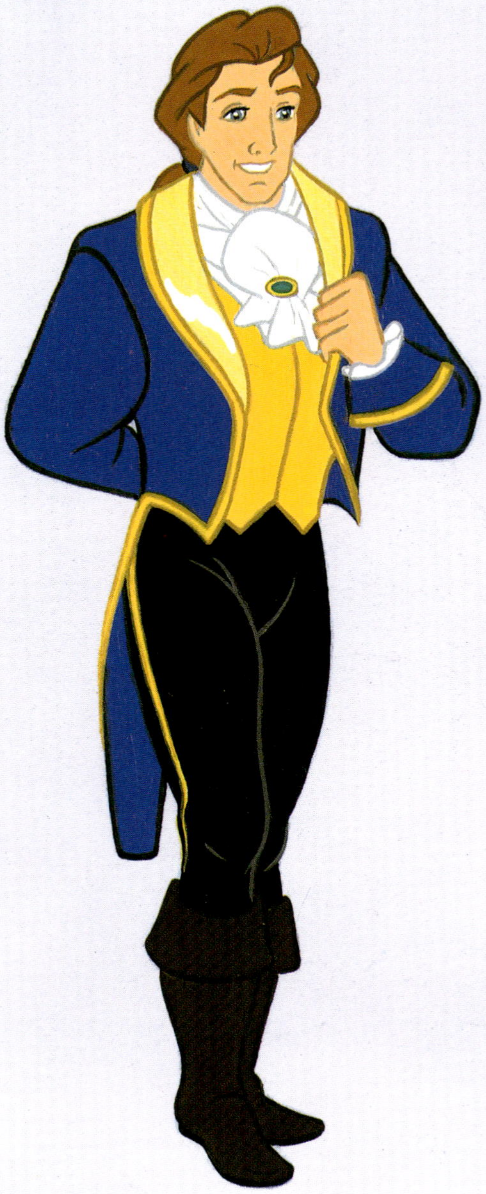

Prince

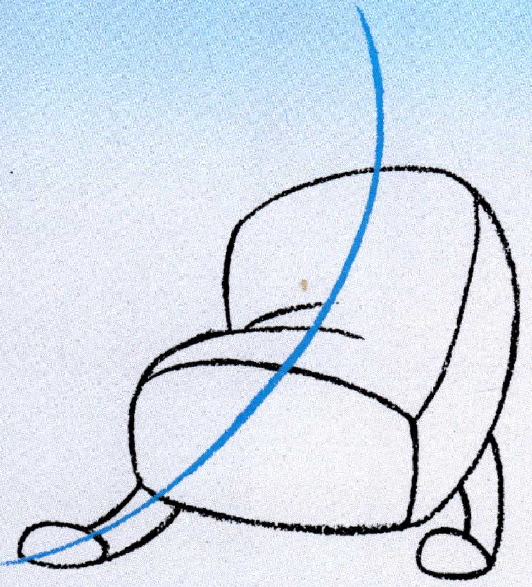

Footstool

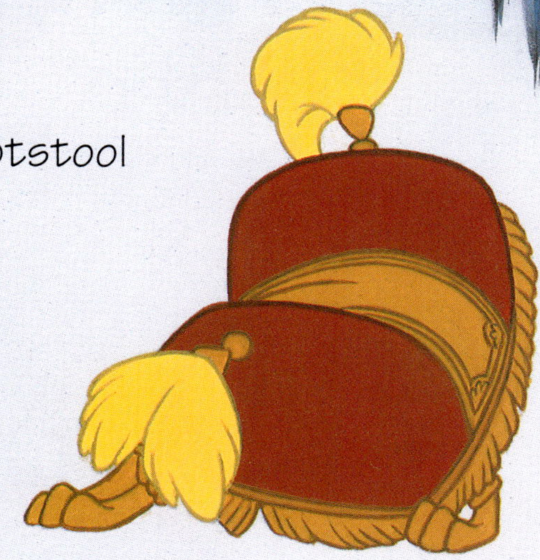

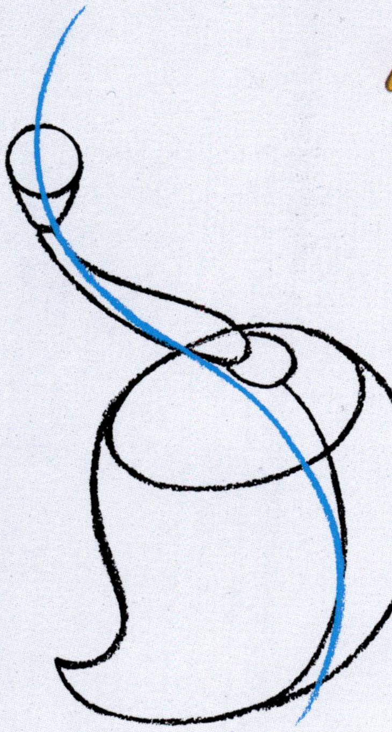

Feather Duster

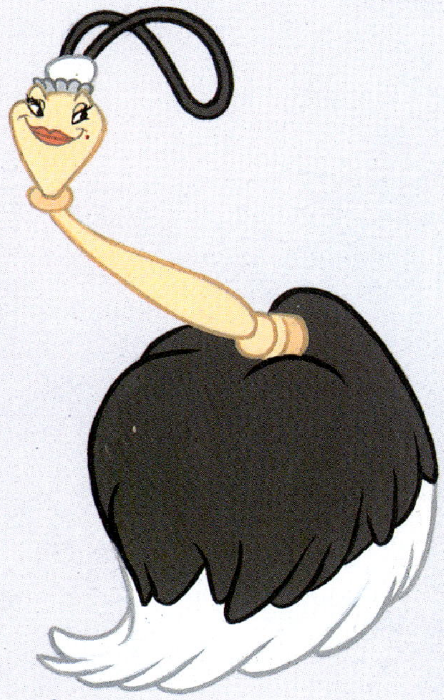

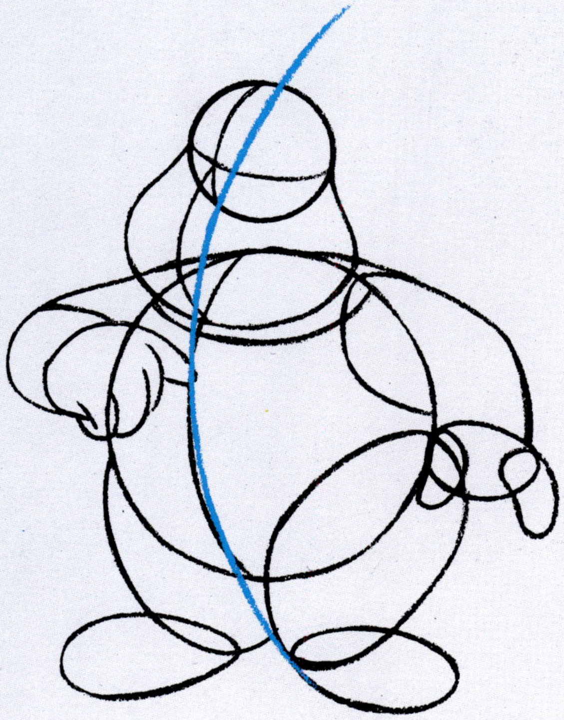

LeFou

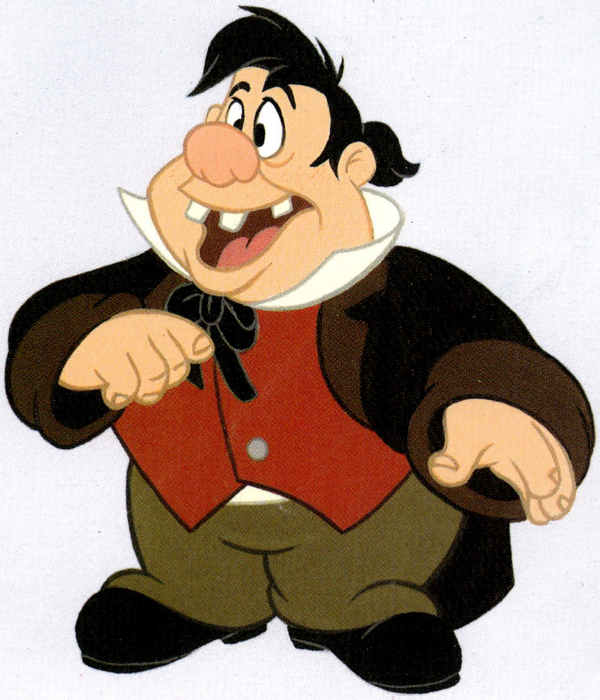

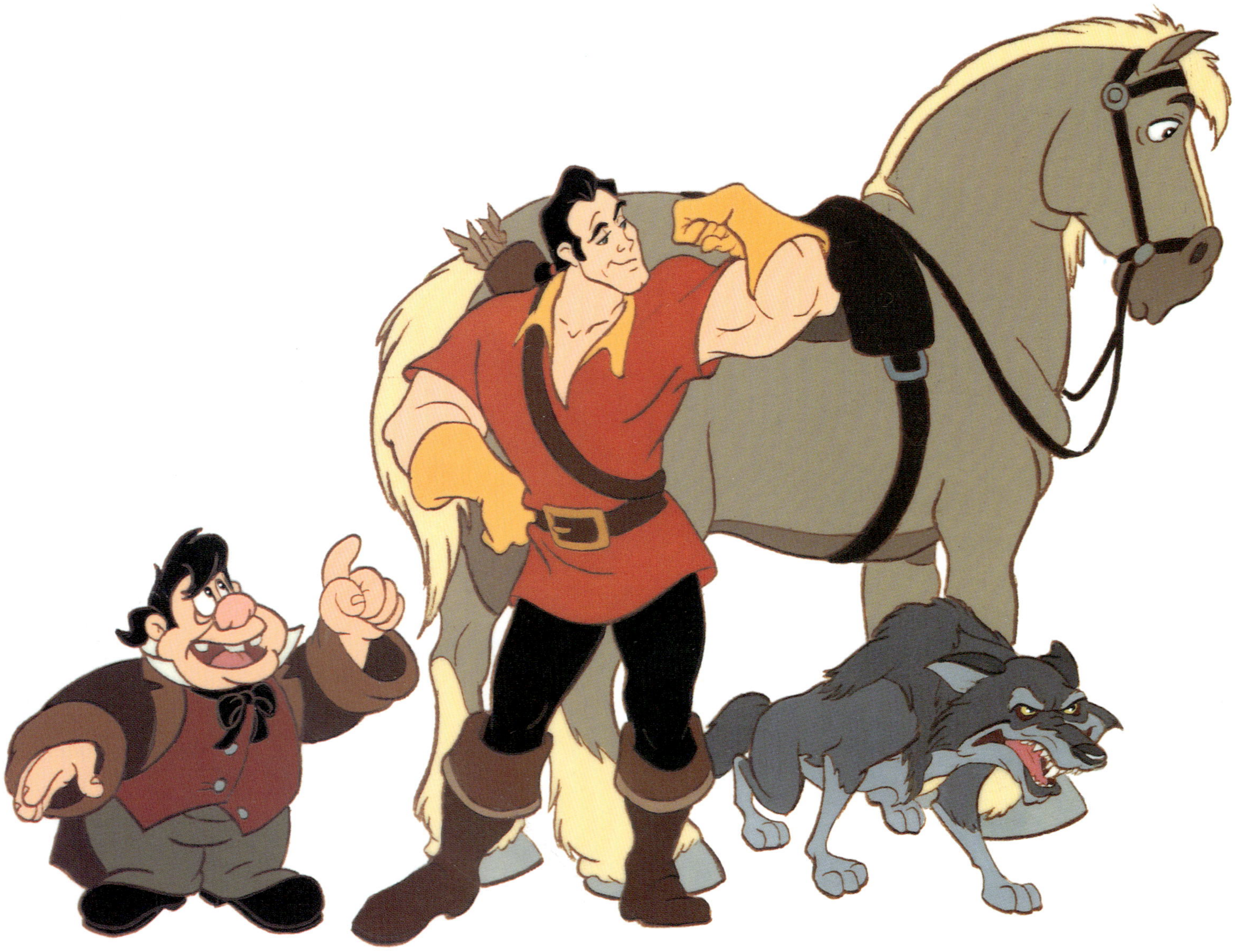